In my experience, most managers sinc
of their people's development. They te
like amateurs at the job. Lisa Koss is a wonderful guide – knowledgeable,
thoughtful, generous, and clear. She has created a treasure-trove of a book
that will help you feel significantly more capable in this role. When you
finish you'll not only want to thank her, you'll be ready to do so in the best
way you can – by paying it forward!

Dr. Robert Kegan
Harvard Professor of Professional Development
and Co-Author of An Everyone Culture

Frankly speaking, I love this book. In my long career in high-tech, I recognize that this approach is the fabric for numerous anecdotal things I've
learned over the years, and it includes many topics that I've not seen before
in print. This book is a sound foundation and framework that ties it all
together in a very logical, very repeatable process, which can subsequently
help organizations get results and drive growth in our business. Going
forward, I certainly plan to keep this model next to me. And I enjoyed this
book, delighted at how the book interweaves aspects of Lisa's fascinating
personal life and journey. I wish she had written this book 30 years ago, so
I might have found it earlier in my career.

Brian Hoerl
Senior Vice President, Global Sales
Mercury Systems

Koss takes coaching practice to the next level with her focus on the
"manager-coach." They will thank her for this very practical and applicable
guide to coaching. Most impressive were her insights on accelerating trust:
the oft-missed, requisite foundation necessary to develop others. I have
rarely seen better.

Mary Ann Rainey, PhD
Co-Editor of Gestalt Practice: Living and
Working in Pursuit of wHolism *(2019)*
and Co-Chair of the iGold program

It's as if Lisa is by your side, encouraging you to experiment, exploring your own motivations about why you want to be a coach/are a coach, and firmly but gently insisting you find your own voice and style. Lisa has written this in a way that coaches you, as you learn to be a coach for others, taking nothing for granted, from the establishment of trust through to the point of letting go of who you were as a coach before reading the book, to the confident coach you have become. Lisa's extensive cross-cultural experiences infused her writing in a way that is easy to read and makes you feel like you have a trusted guide you can turn to when you need additional support. If you are just starting out, or if you are an experienced coach, this book will provide you with either a well laid out roadmap, or the helpful reminders you've been looking for to take your coaching to the next level. We've rolled out this coaching approach across the globe, and are thrilled to now have her insights all in one book.

Karen Lutz
Vice President of Talent and Leadership Development
Xylem Inc.

Leading for Learning is a very distinctive book and thought piece for managers in the post-COVID world. Lisa Koss' practices and wisdom glow through every chapter. Her work is an evolutionary step forward for leaders in the context of new uncertainties who need to accomplish seemingly impossible goals. What I appreciate most about the guidance and these practices is how she clearly outlines the art form and deep gestalt of what it means for managers to be self-aware of their own needs, interests, and wants, and how to engage and motivate others to accomplish their own AND collective goals. Like a master conductor channeling the potential of individual musicians of a symphony, *Leading for Learning* illuminates how a manager can coach and unleash the magic of human motivation, energy, and intelligence of those they lead.

Karen Walch, PhD
Emeritus, Thunderbird School of Global Management

Leading for Learning

Leading for Learning

How Managers Can Get Business Results
through Developmental Coaching and
Inspire Deep Employee Commitment

Lisa J. Koss

Routledge
Taylor & Francis Group

A PRODUCTIVITY PRESS BOOK

First published 2021
by Routledge
6000 Broken Sound Parkway NW, Suite 300, Boca Raton, FL 33487-2742

and by Routledge
2 Park Square, Milton Park, Abingdon, Oxon, OX14 4RN

Routledge is an imprint of the Taylor & Francis Group, an informa business

ISBN: 978-0-367-36936-1 (hbk)
ISBN: 978-0-367-53483-7 (pbk)
ISBN: 978-0-429-35234-8 (ebk)

Typeset in Garamond
by codeMantra

Contents

Acknowledgments

I've never formally introduced myself as "a coach." For 25 years I've called myself an organizational/leadership development consultant and a Gestalt-trained process consultant, but – until recently – have never tied myself to the word. So, to write an entire book on the topic is not what I would have predicted for myself. On the other hand, this is not a book about coaching. It's a book about leadership. Ultimately, I am describing a leadership philosophy reflected in coaching, one of the most powerful dialogic practices available to leaders. Infused with the wisdoms of Gestalt theory, my goal was to find the ideal balance among know-how, inspiration, and pragmatism, to support leaders in bringing more awareness and learning to their workplaces.

This book, thus, is dedicated to all those leaders who I've had the pleasure to know and work with, who strive every day to do their best and achieve their fullest potential as people leaders and as human beings. So many leaders have courageously experimented in our coaching program over the last 10 years and have changed the world for the better, one conversation at a time. This fact must be celebrated and respected because there is much at stake, and as my dear colleague and friend, Karen Walch, says, "Their ass is always on the line!"

Karen has been my "big brain" champion since we first met, and is always eager to know what I've been thinking about and learning, ready to join in and share her insights, wisdom, and enormous encouragement. Her personal and professional guidance has shaped this book, and me.

My sincere appreciation goes to our Ontos coaching faculty around the world, who believe in this work, who have trusted us as partners, who have traveled to remote corners and worked in multiple languages, and who have facilitated and coached so well. Their insights and quotes can be found in these pages.

A specific individual, Christy Valencia, has been a key decision-maker and influencer for many years in her organization, and this book would likely not have been written had she not supported our program as she did, and continues to do. Thank you, Christy.

I also send gratitude to all those, too many to name, who have supported me professionally and personally, in a myriad of ways. Creative energy relies on the generosity and goodness of its ecosystem. I've never been so humbled by this truth as I am today.

Teri Lyn, my dear friend for 30 years, encouraged me throughout the writing of this book, especially through the final effort, demonstrating strength, grace, and intellect without fail.

Finally, I'm ever indebted to David, who has inspired me on every level, including to put this book out into the world.

Author

Lisa J. Koss

For more than 25 years, Lisa has been working at the intersection of individual, team, and organizational transformation. As partner and co-founder of Ontos Global LLC, she helps her clients become more effective change agents through increased self-awareness, leadership presence, resiliency, and capacity to act wisely and decisively despite complex and uncertain times.

Among her key roles at Ontos Global, Lisa is chief designer for all core executive leadership development programs and managing partner for Ontos' global faculty. She is the author of the Developmental Coaching Model (DCM) presented in this book and designer of the accompanying coaching workshop. Her current research in social boundary phenomenon – identifying what it takes to disrupt siloes and transform organizations – has been presented to audiences on four continents.

Lisa consults across geographies and sectors, with mature organizations as well as startups. Her clients include GE, ITT, Xylem, BP, Kaiser Permanente, Bull Information Systems (Atos), Ernst & Young, TATA, Heifer Project International, Honeywell, Pentair, and Mercury Systems, among many others.

She has served as faculty of two executive MBA programs, at the Thunderbird School of Global Management and Instituto Tecnológico de Estudios Superiores de Occidente (Guadalajara, Mexico), and for many years represented ethical consulting as a National Trustee and Chapter President of the Institute of Management Consultants (IMC-USA).

Her doctoral studies at Fielding Graduate University, put on hold as she wrote this book, were preceded by post-graduate studies centered on Gestalt psychology as applied to organizations. Lisa earned her Professional Certified Coach credential in 2010 from the International Coaching Federation.

Having lived abroad seven times and on three continents, her global perspective is core to her identity. She works in English, Spanish, and French, and speaks basic Russian. She currently resides in the San Francisco Bay Area in California.

For more info, see www.ontosglobal.com.

Introduction

If we treat people as they are, we make them worse. If we treat them as they ought to be, we help them to become what they are capable of becoming.

— **Goethe**

Olivia's Case

"Henry" is a talented and hard-working project manager who finds himself increasingly frustrated because, despite his efforts, his team is not completing their deliverables on time. The missed deadlines are affecting the morale of the team, as well as Henry's confidence in his own abilities as a leader. He's begun to work extremely long hours and finds himself spending extra time redoing work his team members hurriedly submit. Henry's energy is waning. He wonders where all this will end up, because there are only so many hours in a day.

Olivia is Henry's manager. Olivia is also feeling increased pressure in her role due to recent financial results. Her manager wants Olivia to "coach Henry." Olivia has been supporting Henry in different ways, but as she sits again with Henry to ask about his team's results, she starts to wonder whether Henry is the right person for the role. As usual, she asks questions to determine what's happening in his team and gives pointed advice about what could be done differently. As before, Henry tries to implement her advice but real progress remains elusive. With every one step forward, there seems to be another step back. Olivia is not sure what else to do besides finding a project manager with more experience.

Perhaps you can relate to Olivia, Henry, or both. You wonder why people can't take good advice or simply figure it out. You drag your feet before these one-on-one sit-downs with direct reports, wondering how to deliver the message. Or you find yourself stepping in to solve the issue yourself as your frustration increases, and all the while wondering what you're missing. How to work more effectively with "Henry"?

I wrote this book because I was an "Olivia" of sorts. In my case, it was early in my consulting career, and I needed to be more effective with a client. The client, "Leo," was the Director of Operations in Mexico, a manufacturing facility near the U.S. border in Mexico. I'd been consulting for him for some time when he asked me to design and facilitate a strategy retreat with his team – half the members were Mexican and half American. I was happy to do it; the context was interesting given my research and work with multicultural teams, I had extensive experience in facilitation, leading strategy sessions, and was fluent in Spanish.

Given the size of the team, I needed a partner and so hired a trusted and experienced colleague, Jeanne Schulze, and we facilitated a quality, 2-day, strategy session. In the evening, Jeanne and I gathered with the team to celebrate the session's success and relax. Near the end of the evening, the director took me and Jeanne aside. He began sharing a new issue, clearly looking for advice. I responded while Jeanne looked on, but I will always remember Jeanne's reaction after Leo walked away. Looking directly at me, she said, "Lisa, you don't coach a client that way!" I had no idea what she was talking about.

Why You Should Read This Book

In the spirit of coaching, allow me to turn this question around and ask why are you interested in this book? What's motivating you? What are you looking to achieve? Why does that matter to you? What will that change? How might you benefit? By clearly identifying your reasons for reading, you are raising your self-awareness, just as you will be asking your coachees to do. Consider how much motivation to coach you have currently, what you hope to learn, and what you have to gain with this new skillset. The following 4 reasons are intended to get your juices flowing.

As a People Manager, You're Expected to Coach Others

As one advances in one's career, becoming a people manager is often an organizational expectation. For most, this sits well for a variety of reasons. First, "managing others" reflects a certain success or status perhaps because others have been entrusted to us. At a minimum, we like the idea of someone else doing the work we don't want to do. Second, we like the fact that more can be accomplished in the same amount of time. Moreover, most managers care about their people and want them to do well. On the other hand, despite all these positives, there is a certain ambivalence about taking on the responsibilities that come with the role. We hear: "Is developing others really my job?" or "No one coached *me* and I figured it out!" An ideal employee, in other words, is frequently thought of as someone who understands his role entirely and executes consistently and with minimal errors. He is efficient, effective, and low maintenance. Sooner or later, a palpable ambivalence emerges about the responsibility required to develop others. A certain dragging of feet, even resentment, results from the amount of commitment developing others really takes.

This book then, is a response to those who feel curious, confused, or ambivalent on the question "Is developing others really my job?" With very few exceptions, the answer is an unequivocal YES. Accepting the position of people leader means supporting the lives and careers of those that work for you. The problem is many managers are not clear on the implications of becoming a people manager, and have not been properly prepared to take on the role. Managers, in many organizations, are expected to magically know how to lead and coach others without instruction, guiding principles, or tools. This book addresses these gaps, and, given our diverse and global workplaces, incorporates strategies that work across cultures.

You Have Nagging People and Business Issues

Some may be interested in this book as a means to address ongoing concerns about particular individuals and related business issues. Communication feels particularly difficult for these "Henry situations," and despite best efforts to explain, suggest, and provide advice, the response is not as hoped. These managers ask themselves why their employees can't figure it out, or take advice, especially since others have been there before, learned the hard way, and have insights to share. The feeling that builds up often subconsciously is an experience of personal failure. The manager feels they've tried many avenues to resolve the issue. As the frustration mounts, so does the anxiety and the blame. These managers may begin to conflate their struggles with the organization as a whole, wondering how they can be expected to deal with so many people issues and why HR can't play a larger role in finding better candidates in the first place. Still unsatisfied, they ask themselves, "What am I missing?"

This book is for those who would like to get better at turning around nagging people and business issues by learning a methodology to have dramatically better conversations, changing the dialogue from blame to one of sustainable solutions.

You Want to Become a Guide for Others

Some managers have reached a point in life and career when their attention turns to an altruistic motivation to share what they've learned, tell their stories, help others understand, and pass on hard-earned wisdoms. They like the idea of helping someone be successful and guiding them so that they can avoid painful lessons. It feels good and important to help others in the way that they were helped (or perhaps not) along the way. They know that organizations don't change, people do.

Another audience for this book, then, is those who want to enable others' success. The question, however, is how to best do this, because caring is not the same as being effective. Everyone has their own ideas and experiences, but what are the skills required to develop others and do it well?

You Need People to Learn Faster and Systematically

Some managers are acutely aware of the enormous shifts now taking place in the work environment, shifts which have been happening since the middle of the last century, called by some as the Digital Revolution or the Fourth Age of Industrialization.[1] Says the Founder and Executive Chairman of the World Economic Forum, Klaus Schwab: "The combining of advanced technologies is leading to disruption everywhere – in almost every industry, in every country, transforming entire systems of production, management, and governance." The exponential pace means that fewer aspects of organizations can be "managed"; there is too much to know and too much to do. Instead, adapting to ongoing change will require learning continuously and more rapidly. Peter Senge, a systems scientist and a major figure in the field of organizational development, developed the notion of a learning organization. In his book, called by the *Harvard Business Review* as one of the most seminal management books in the last 75 years, he concluded that "over the long run, superior performance depends on superior learning."[2] This suggests the need to rethink the work leaders are called to do.

This book, then, is also written for those who feel compelled to respond to these macroeconomic shifts. They realize their organizations are not well prepared to let go of control, to access a diversity of people or approaches, nor to adequately embrace the change and disruption happening all around them. They see coaching as an important leadership practice to help people rethink assumptions, stimulate curiosity, and accelerate learning.

So, why are *you* reading? Your answer to this question will generate the energy to take the next step. Examine your personal motivations: What can you gain by learning to coach? In which ways could coaching others be exceptionally rewarding? What would you expect to feel as you learn to guide others to success? In what ways is it important for you to bring diverse perspectives forward? Are you motivated to make a difference in people's lives? Are you inspired to fundamentally change what your organization prioritizes? Articulating what you want and why that motivates you is what coaches ask their clients. You can ask yourself the same.

A Coaching Skillset and Mindset

The goal of this book is to make the case – and provide the tools – to become a "manager-coach," which means having both a *skillset and a mindset* that embraces development as a strategy for sustainable growth and scalability. Coaching is a *skillset* because the coaching process is eminently learnable and applied; you'll learn a set of seven steps that will guide your conversation. Through experimentation, you'll learn the mechanics and discover your own coaching style, while becoming more aware of the nuances and dynamics of relationships, change, and learning.

Coaching is also a *mindset* because coaching skills work best when aligned to corresponding, underlying, developmental principles. At the broadest level, for example, the model has embedded the principles of democratic decision-making, participatory social interactions, individual empowerment, personal/professional development, and mutual reliance and accountabilities. (To be clear, coaching can work in any society, but living in an environment of free speech, for example, can make it easier for one to get one's needs met.) In addition, for those familiar with Gestalt psychology, you'll see a strong connection in this book with that body of work. In fact, Gestalt theory and practice is a major inspiration for this book.[3] Let's look now at several core mindsets that you'll see integrated throughout the chapters.

Coaching Mindset #1: Developing Others Means Developing Oneself

That any person aspires to meaningfully impact another suggests the need for great humility and responsibility. The notion that people voluntarily come to their places of work to fulfill their role with their knowledge, skill, and dedication *in addition to* their hopes, dreams, and potential is to deeply recognize that all people want to live in happiness and fulfillment, and to develop to the greatest extent they can. This is a reminder that leadership entails an orientation to service, that workplaces can be environments of self-actualization, and the need for managers to engage the whole person.

Managers can only be helpful in this endeavor to the extent that they appreciate others' aspirations as they do their own, and have the ability to unleash others' potential through an authentic presence and a sufficiently broad repertoire of skills. For example, can the manger-coach speak about one's thoughts *and* feelings? Share with others transparently *and* intentionally? Decipher when to save time *and* when to invest time? In effect, being credible as a manager-coach requires the same eagerness to learn, just as they ask others to do. An aspiring manager-coach doesn't need to be perfect; we are ALL a work in progress, but the willingness to keep developing oneself is the most foundational criterion of all.

Coaching Mindset #2: Cultivating Curiosity about Others

Curiosity is a fundamental requirement for a coach because it's the doorway to learning. Curiosity is defined as "the desire for new information that results in exploration and new knowledge."[4] Whether a coach or client, when we become curious, we are inviting an interruption, of sorts, to the programs encoded in our brains. Metaphorically speaking, we become open to updating our operating system and rewriting some of that code. Coaches need to interrupt their assumptions and projections as much as clients do. Going one step further than curiosity, coaches need the ability to wonder. Wondering is different than curiosity because it's a precursor to the cognitive realm. Wonder is deeply felt in the body, emanating from an internal state of truly not knowing. Asking questions from an unfamiliar place supports an environment of non-judgment and trust.

Some are more curious (or more full of wonder) than others, of course, and everyone has their favorite domain(s) of curiosity – tasks, things, concepts, people, etc. For aspiring manager-coaches, becoming highly interested in *people* will help managers stay true to the purpose of coaching. This is not to say that those who are more curious in other areas cannot be excellent coaches, but finding the bridge to being interested in *who* people are and *why* they do what they do more easily changes the focus away from "let's-fix-this-issue-as-quickly-as-possible" toward those of "let's-learn-who-you-are-and-who-you-want-to-be."

Coaching Mindset #3: Resistance Is the Answer, Not the Problem

Because coaching inherently incorporates the concept of change, coaches can expect to experience resistance from their clients, as well as from inside themselves. The term "resistance," unfortunately, tends to have a negative connotation when, in fact, it refers to a phenomenon which is entirely healthy and natural, necessary for humans to survive and thrive. We need resistance, for example, to not succumb to some of our very own ideas. Consider the experience of reaching for an unfamiliar dog. Some of our own ideas – and the unfamiliar dog – represent options we may turn away from, but turning toward or turning away both have their merit. As such, a manager-coach can translate resistance as something to engage with and understand. Resistance as a concept loses its threat and becomes an opportunity to learn. In fact, the very notion of resisting something at all could be characterized as "integrity, because it entails acting in accordance with one's beliefs."[5] With this frame of reference, honoring one's own – and others' – resistance becomes a matter of probity, necessitating respect, and an essential ethos of becoming a manager-coach.

And lest we forget, humans are perfectly adaptable to make the choices that meet their needs. Internal resistance guides us in important ways. Despite the many choices that present themselves each day, people are not broken; they've adapted when it made sense in the past, and can do so again, given amenable conditions. You've perhaps heard the axiom: People don't resist change, only *being* changed. Feeling resistance means you've encountered something meaningful, signaling the opportunity for more awareness, but also that people are both capable, and clearly in the best position, to choose their own path.

Various resistances are at play for the manager as well, and an object of exploration and discovery. One common tension is the desire to control the outcome while paradoxically wanting the coachee to take charge of his own development. The internal resistance is understandable in hierarchical and economic structures where managers are paid to achieve predetermined outcomes but, as we will see, intrinsic motivation is unquestionably more useful long term.

A Global Perspective and Approach

One of the objectives of this book is to incorporate perspectives, strategies, and examples that reflect the traditions of both the East and the West.[6] It goes (almost) without saying that diverse and global workforces have become the norm and managers need approaches and tools that correspond. Gone are the days to use regional or country-based typologies to guide our communication and interaction with others, because while typologies help raise awareness about different ways of perceiving and behaving, they aren't very useful in the moment of conversation.

Despite the positive reception of this model from managers around the world, questions might emerge about the very premise of this book. For example, one embedded assumption is that an employee would find it useful to discuss their personal or professional development with one's manager that includes elements of explicit feedback. A prior coaching client of mine, for example, a Chinese sales director residing near Shanghai, explained that giving direct feedback was very rare in his experience. In fact, he felt that asking his manager for feedback would be much too risky. "Why?" I asked. "Because," he responded, "if she wanted to give me feedback, she already would have. And if she didn't want to give me feedback and I were to ask her anyway, it could lead to embarrassment because she hadn't wanted to provide it. We would then both be aware of this fact for the entire length of our relationship." These social norms of why, when, and with whom to discuss feedback are distinct from my own, and I continued in curiosity, "Is there ever a justification for providing feedback to another?" "Not really. Leaders teach by being role models," he replied. "The employee must observe and reflect on what they see and adapt to that as a model of success." "But," I insisted, "what if the coachee never makes the effort, despite a positive role model? How long would it take before a manager might feel compelled to provide feedback more directly?" "Not sure," he replied, "maybe 7 years."

When and how to use the coaching approach described in this book must always be considered in light of the cultural context: Nothing is straightforward or unidimensional. Despite the above anecdote, for example, this coaching approach and model has been very well received in China (and has been delivered many times in both Mandarin and English). This model attempts to balance different world views. On one hand, for example, coaches and clients are prompted to look inside themselves for answers – the "truth" of a situation for any individual does not reside somewhere "out there," waiting to be found. Connecting to oneself – who one is, how one feels, and what one wants – makes coaching more personally grounding than other management approaches.[7] On the other hand, staying open to others and incorporating external information means gaining new insights. The intention of this model, then, is to balance internal and external wisdom in a context of trust, as well as to expose underlying needs and motivations, important with diverse actors when assumptions about others are especially prone to be incorrect.

Does This Method Work?

At the time of this writing, the Developmental Coaching Model (DCM) has been taught to over 2,000 people managers on 5 continents and in 16 countries. Translated and taught in nine languages, feedback from the program has been consistently high, attaining an "A" rating of 94% "overall effectiveness" across all groups, regions, and languages, and across all clients.[8] The DCM is the center-piece of a 2-day coaching workshop, entitled "Manager-as-Coach I" (now with a follow-up, "Manager-as-Coach II", adding an emphasis on conflict management and diversity). "Manager-as-Coach Online" was launched in 2020. It all began as a pilot at a manufacturing facility in Mexico in 2009 as part of a leadership development program, and later became a stand-alone workshop at Ontos for an engineering team for a global client. The success of the program spread virally across the organization, and the company took notice, enlisting the pro-gram as a component of their leadership development for all people leaders.

Many have attested that the coaching process has significantly improved their relationships, making them more effective leaders. One leader recently reported that he estimates the financial impact to be $1 million in rev-enue for his business because when his leadership team used the model to engage their own teams he was able to successfully transition his focus to building out a new market segment. Others have said they use the coach-ing model in unforeseen (to us) ways: organizing the flow of presentations, designing a process for group discussions, even improving communication with their kids. One client, Rebecca Jacqua, regularly checks in with us, call-ing the workshop "a spa for the brain" and saying she gets tangible results with every coaching session.

The Origins of Coaching, Briefly

Before we move to the "how" of coaching, it can be useful to understand how coaching came to be. Where does it come from? On what theoretical ground does it stand? What follows is a brief (if somewhat reductionist) look at the origins of coaching followed by how it links to the big ideas behind our model.

Coaching was spawned from an expanded field of study which garnered new attention after World War II, changing the nature of organizations forever: management science.[9] This new science intended to make management "rigorous, scientific, quantitative" with tools and research instead of guesswork, personal judgment, and personal experience. Ideas, methods, and tools emerged in all realms: quality, inventory control, continuous improvement, financial management, and more – much of which enabled the organization to minimize or eliminate risk. These all had an enormous impact on efficiency and cost savings in the following decades and continue to do so to this day.

Paradoxically, the main goal of management science was to enable individuals to take the right risk, and *greater* risks, given the availability and enhanced quality of information.[10] But in some ways, the science was sorely lacking. What was lost in the search for the effective organization was the fact that organizations are made up of *human beings*. Management science had all but left the study of humans to the side. Meanwhile, the social sciences – sociology, psychology, and anthropology – were developing theories about the nature of individuals, groups, and social systems, but these were rarely integrated into management sciences. This was unfortunate as the real challenges in organizations were to better understand the complex reality of leaders, to provide models and tools to enhance the conceptual reality of people to foster communication and collective inquiry.[11] Renown management guru, Peter Drucker, drew attention to this fact years later: "the assumptions, opinions, objectives, and even errors of people (and especially of managers) – [are] the facts for the management scientist."[12]

Among the social psychologists who helped the world put a more human frame of reference on the topic was Douglas McGregor from the MIT Sloan School of Management. His seminal research in the 1950s called for rethinking how managers approach humans at work, coining the terms simply "Theory X" and "Theory Y."[13] Theory X called out the prevailing assumption at the time – that humans are naturally passive and resistant, work as little as possible, lack ambition, and are self-centered. "Theory X" managers use terminology such as "firm but fair" and ask people to do as they're told and to minimize resistance through explanations and other forms of persuasion. Certain approaches to performance appraisals could be considered Theory X, similar to the process of testing equipment on the production floor: a regular inspection complete with diagnosis at scheduled intervals, whereby certain parts need to be changed out or maybe a decision made to buy a whole new machine. Theory X had to be in force, McGregor argued, given the conventional management practice: Direct them, motivate through extrinsic means, control through persuasion, reward, and punish. In sum, people must be closely managed in order for the organization to reach its goals.

"Theory Y," on the other hand, was based on an entirely different assumption. Humans, the theory went, are not at all passive, nor resistant, to organizational needs. Humans *want* to do good work and *want* to succeed, because they are naturally inclined to do so.[14] The manager's essential task, then, is to create the conditions and methods which allow people to direct their own efforts in service to the organization's objectives.[15]

McGregor overlaid the research on motivation with that of social psychologist Abraham Maslow. Maslow's "hierarchy of needs" suggested motivations change over time and depend on the individual's developmental phase. At one time, someone might have the greatest need for safety – personal security, employment, resources, health, property, etc. At another, the greatest need might be for social connectedness, friendship, and intimacy. At another, the greatest need might be for respect, self-esteem, status, recognition, strength, and freedom. At another, motivation could be for self-actualization due to a yearning for what one was meant to be in life.[16] The theory goes that for any given individual, once a category of need is met, the next-level need becomes the focus. How a manager engages with each person in regards to development would change accordingly. Managers who make assumptions about what is motivational for a given person (pay, conditions, benefits, steady employment, etc.) are likely incorrect.[17] And no matter that later research does not fully support all of Maslow's theory, its relevance for coaching is intact: "A satisfied need is not a motivator of behavior."[18] In other words, creating the conditions for people to be successful means staying aware of their motivation as it changes over time.

CAN YOU CHANGE WHAT MOTIVATES?

On the day I write this, an example emerges from a frustrated manager. In seeking a coach for one of her employees she said, "I just want her to stop focusing on titles and whether she is getting enough respect. I'd like her to focus on continuing her good work and the enjoyment of working with a great group of people." In essence, her manager would like her to be motivated differently. But changing what motivates is not the idea of coaching.

Decades later, the business sector is still slow to incorporate the conclusions from the social sciences. Many managers still hold – certainly unconsciously – to the Industrial Age idea that we should manage people similarly to how we manage things: Is success measured by measuring human efficiency or output? Should we change out people like parts on a production line by acting quickly and make bold changes when seeing too much failure? Should we think about people like other assets – short-term or long-term "investments" based on one's current value and/or future potential? These questions seem at odds with our more complex times. The science has shown that these frames of reference are shortsighted and ineffective. To return to the two anecdotes presented at the beginning of this Introduction – Olivia with Henry, or myself with Leo – neither coaching client was adequately engaged to link motivations, resistances, and aspirations to the broader organizational context. Without these, all we have left is short-term problem solving. Jeanne's declaration, "Lisa, you don't coach a client that way!" was an important feedback for me to continue to learn and develop.

What This Book Is *Not*

Professional coaches have told us that the model has improved their coaching, as it does ours. But this book is not intended to correspond to all the considerations and standards for professional coaches. This book is written for people managers. The following describes what's different about being a manager-coach:

1. *Managers have a stake in outcomes.* The formal and informal power structure inherent in organizations often makes it unrealistic for the manager to be as unbiased as external, professional coaches can be.

Managers have a personal interest in many decisions employees make, especially since achievement of the managers' own goals depends directly on employee results. When coaching, managers will find themselves feeling the need to choose between achieving business outcomes and development of the person.

2. *Organizations put pressure on managers for quick fixes.* Managers must deal with the temptation to address day-to-day issues and reduce developmental conversations to quick problem-solving. It's easier for professional coaches to stay out of these traps, keeping the individual client's long-term personal and professional development as the center of concern.

3. *Conflicts of interest create unexpected outcomes.* Achieving a trusting relationship can be more complex for a manager. Imagine all the scenarios which influence whether an employee shares openly, such as a concern about the manager's intentions or the organization's true commitment to employee development. I had a coaching client, for example, who believes her own role was eliminated during a reorganization because she had transparently shared with her manager her concerns about her own role-fit. While no one but the decision-maker in that case will know for sure, organizations are nothing if not pragmatic.

4. *Limited skills working with emotional and psychological subject matter.* Professional coaches usually have had extensive coaching training and experience that support clients in navigating deeper, psychological dilemmas. Consider the challenge for managers of tackling issues of self-esteem or fear of failure without an adequate orientation to those domains. Even if individuals are intensely motivated to change, underlying psychological fears often block progress. A manager may be more limited in her skills to work with these dynamics.

The model and approach directly address these managerial realities. You'll find strategies to navigate the complexities, while always maintaining a focus on what's in the client's best interest.

WHAT'S THE DIFFERENCE BETWEEN COACHING AND MENTORING?

Mentoring is often confused with coaching. While the concepts do overlap in that both intend to support a client to learn, the approach is very different. A mentor typically guides by sharing what she's learned over time – her career, leadership lessons, or information pertaining to a specific context or situation. Mentoring tends to consist of advice on specific topics or situations. Coaching is process-based, meaning that a coach guides a person through his *own* thought process, reviewing his *own* experiences and learnings, and helps the coachee shape his goals and development, using a combination of challenge and support.

Book Summary by Chapter

To read this book is to hopefully become inspired to achieve the rewards of integrating the principles of skillset and mindset in becoming a manager-coach. In its six chapters, this book begins by setting broad context (Chapter 1), introduces the Developmental Coaching Model (DCM) (Chapter 2), and then devotes one chapter for each of the three phases of the DCM (Chapter 3, 4, and 5). The last chapter is application and the establishment of sustainable behavior change through changing formal and informal practices (Chapter 6).

This book is meant to be highly practical and applied, providing a guide to managers who want to achieve much more in their conversations: to engage others in their own development, build deeper respect and trust, and to get business results at the same time.

Chapter 1 begins with "What's the Big Deal about Coaching?" providing the rationale for developmental coaching. In this section, common questions on the topic of coaching are enumerated; they are answered in the following chapters. "Developmental coaching" is defined, including the unique set of factors that make developing a coaching skillset more relevant today than ever before. Among the factors is the notion of increased productivity through "discretionary effort," the significant payback available to those able to successfully engage others in a holistic way, including motivations and aspirations. Another factor is that of developing "psychological flexibility," a kind of learning acumen required in this modern age when the future is more uncertain than ever. The ability to pay attention to more phenomenon, track patterns, raise self-awareness, and reexamine assumptions, is foundational in becoming more agile. The chapter ends with a variation on the Henry/Olivia case study seen in the Introduction (a preview of what is in store relative to the coaching process) and the four key elements that coaches track while they coach.

Chapter 2, "The Developmental Coaching Model," describes how this coaching model is different and why it matters. The DCM is specifically for people managers, designed to be grounded in real-life complexities of the modern workplace, but also with an aspirational premise for those who are truly motivated to make a difference at either the individual, organizational, or societal level. The Gestalt notion of resistance is explored in some detail, as well as the complementary topic of motivation, both concepts central to every chapter of this book. The model's success around the world in 9 languages during the last 10 years is reviewed. Turning to the model itself, the three phases and seven steps are summarized. Also see comments about the use of the model with one's peers or manager, in addition to one's direct reports. The end of the chapter is meant to remind the reader about the importance of practice. Experimenting with the method and techniques will turn information into experience, and then experience into coaching skills.

Chapter 3, "Build Trust," pertains to the first phase of coaching. Other coaching models relegate trust to the background, as purely context. In this model trust is promoted into the foreground as a step – "Establish a Climate of Trust" – to provide a visual reminder of two important facts: (1) If you want to coach someone where there is little or no trust, you'll need to focus on that first; and (2) at the beginning and during a coaching conversation there's a lot a coach can do to foster ease, openness, and collaboration which can further weave trust into the fabric of the relationship and contribute to the learning and business results. The chapter begins with a commentary on the complexity of trust. It provides two rules as well as reflections on the rate at which trust develops. The chapter concludes with ways to accelerate trust-building, and strategies to mitigate five trust challenges.

Chapter 4, "Contracting," covers the second phase of coaching. The term "contracting" refers to a psychological agreement on what the coaching conversation will be about. Contracting is what makes coaching very distinct from other kinds of communication – it's the conversation before the conversation. In Steps #2, 3, and 4, the challenge or business problem is transformed into a developmental conversation, linking the client's motivations and resistances with the organizational context. If explicit agreement on the developmental topic is not reached, then the coach and coachee will exit the coaching process. (The conversation may continue, but it will no longer be coaching.) The role that the coach will play during the conversation is also established. Throughout this chapter, the reader will find many examples and case studies, including scenarios of coach-initiated coaching or client-initiated coaching.

Chapter 5, "Work the Idea/Issue," is the third and final phase of the model. The "idea/issue" is always the developmental opportunity established during the Contracting phase. In Step #5, the coach uses a transition question or statement to begin the process of exploration, and often ends with the coachee identifying potential experiments. Restraint is important for the coach to not solve or over-function, so that the client stays at the center of her own development. In Step #6, the coach may choose to share an experience or guide the coachee in some way, but only as necessary. Finally, in Step #7, the coach and client close the conversation by reflecting together on the conversation itself, attending to several aspects of the conversation.

Chapter 6, "Becoming a Manager-Coach," addresses the challenge of initiating and sustaining a new practice. Through experimentation, managers will build confidence to start new habits. By sticking to practicing the 3 phases of the model managers are literally changing their brains, reinforcing the link between business issues and employee development. The chapter closes by calibrating two common questions: Is coaching used for performance problems? And, what does the manager do when there's no time to coach?

Finally, a note on cases, names, and terminology in this book: While all of the cases presented are based on the author's real experiences, any given case may represent a compilation of more than one. All names of people in this book are fictional. Likewise, the use of "she" and "he" is arbitrary. "Client" and "coachee" are used interchangeably and refer to the person who is being supported by the coach.

Notes

1 Schwab, K. (2019). The fourth industrial revolution: What it means, how to respond. *World Economic Forum*. Retrieved from: https://www.weforum.org/agenda/2016/01/the-fourth-industrial-revolution-what-it-means-and-how-to-respond/.
2 Senge, P. M. (2006). *The Fifth Discipline: The Art and Practice of the Learning Organization*. New York, NY: Doubleday.
3 Those familiar with the principles and practice of Gestalt theory, a core orientation of the author, will recognize its influence in the pages of this book. Gestalt is a German word loosely defined as "whole," and originates from the study of the science of perception. How one perceives impacts the degree of self-, other-, and system-awareness and subsequent decisions and outcomes.
4 Berlyne, D. E. (1954). A theory of human curiosity. *British Journal of Psychology*, *45*(3), 180-191.

5 The idea of linking resistance to integrity comes from Veronica Hopper Carter and John D. Carter, President and CEO of Gestalt Center for Organization & Systems Development.

6 Buddhist and Eastern philosophy and thinking were a primary reference system in Gestalt psychology and Gestalt as applied to organizational systems development.

7 The notion that coaching is "more grounded than other management approaches" comes from: O'Connor, J., & Lages, A. (2009). *How Coaching Works: The Essential Guide to the History and Practice of Effective Coaching.* London: A&C Black.

8 The global average of "overall effective" on a scale of 1-5 by participants on post-workshop feedback forms for workshop "Manager-as-Coach" I and II in Africa, Asia, Europe, North America, and South America.

9 Fredrick Taylor spawned the field in the first part of the 20th century. Principles of Scientific Management was published in 1911.

10 Taking risks reflects the very nature of free enterprise, because profit can only happen by taking risks, and the fact that committing current resources is made in order to meet our hoped-for, desired, future expectations is *also* a risk.

11 See endnote 3.

12 Maslow specified that learning is an important motivator across all of the needs because new information helps us meet any given unsatisfied need. For example, learning about the environment we live in will help reinforce our need for a sense of security. Drucker, P. F. (1974) *Management: Tasks, Responsibilities, Practices.* New York, NY: Harper and Row.

13 By using the nomenclature "X" and "Y," McGregor hoped to avoid labels which can be misleading.

14 McGregor argued it was the experience itself of working in hierarchical organizations which created this undesirable behavior.

15 McGregor, D. M. (1989). The human side of enterprise. In H. J. Leavitt, L.R. Pondy, & D. M. Boje (Eds.), *Readings in Managerial Psychology* (4th Ed., pp. 314–324). Chicago, IL; University of Chicago Press.

16 Hopper, E. (2019, February 25). *Maslow's Hierarchy of Needs Explained.* Retrieved from: https://www.thoughtco.com/maslows-hierarchy-of-needs-4582571.

17 Managers may find that people make demands for lower level needs (for example, more pay) when they perceive no opportunities to fulfill actual needs.

18 McGregor, D. M. (1989). Other theories of motivation include those of "self-determination" (Deci & Ryan); "self-preservation" (Greenberg, Pyszezynsky, & Solomon); "belonging" (Fiske); and the "cognitive-experiential self" (Epstein). For more info see: Van Lange, P. A., De Cremer, D., Van Dijk, E., & Van Vugt, M. (2007). Self-interest and beyond. In A. W. Kruglanski, & E. T. Higgins (Eds.), *Social Psychology: Handbook of Basic Principles* (pp. 540–561). New York, NY: The Guilford Press.

Chapter 1

Developmental Coaching

The wicked leader is one who the people despise. The good leader is one who the people revere.

The great leader is one who the people say, "We did it ourselves."[1]

— Lao Tsu

What's the Big Deal about Coaching?

I suspect if you're reading this, you're already curious about coaching. And you might ask, "What is coaching, really?" You probably know the basic premise – that coaching is about helping others achieve their goals through dialogue. You also may already know – and do – a number of the things associated with quality coaching: Listen carefully to your colleagues about a concerning issue, show interest in others to stimulate a deeper conversation, encourage friends to try something new, or make observations that turn around more banal conversations. Some of these conversations have been rewarding and have deepened trust. Others less so. But in any case, no matter the context, the human experience is defined by exchanges with others that reflect elements of coaching conversations.

So, then, what's the big deal about coaching? Is coaching simply a good conversation with a twist? If so, what's the twist? Perhaps you've heard that coaching includes asking a lot of good questions. (Often true.) Perhaps you've heard that coaching is about getting the other person to come up with his or her own answers. (Generally, yes.) Is coaching about good communication skills? (Yes, it helps.) But while these aspects are useful in many situations, a developmental coach does a lot more.

What Is Developmental Coaching?

The term "coaching" has come to mean many things to different people, so let's describe our intent and provide a definition. First, the coaching approach in this book is geared specifically to *people managers* – those who hire others and have direct responsibility for their performance. This doesn't mean others won't benefit from this book – the model will help anyone build their skills – but the model is specifically designed for those who want to more skillfully coach their direct reports and colleagues in the workplace.

Second, the word "developmental" clarifies the desired outcome. While being a people manager typically includes the responsibility of developing others, in practice many managers think of development as the annual performance review and advice-giving when employees struggle. Meanwhile, the International Coaching Federation (ICF) defines coaching as "partnering with clients in a thought-provoking and creative process that inspires them to maximize their personal and professional potential."[2] To add more description for our purposes, developmental coaching fuses the business topic with employee development by ...

- ... partnering with another ...
- ... in a thought-provoking and creative process ...
- ... to identify and address a developmental dilemma of importance to the coachee and the organization,
- ... embracing resistance as natural and useful, and clarifying the coachee's motivation,
- ... in order to inspire the coachee to maximize her personal and professional potential.

This partnership allows the coachee to ...

- ... discover new choices
- ... take on new challenges
- ... build relationship and trust with the coach
- ... increase a sense of well-being.

Why Developmental Coaching?

The benefits of developmental coaching are perhaps already clear given the Introduction in this book. But the following rationale and accompanying anecdotes will provide a different view than what we've seen thus far.

The Need for Purpose

We need look no further than our own selves to see that people, now more than ever, seek answers that resonate with their own sensibilities. It's highly questionable, for example, whether most people will tolerate being told what to do and how to do it, as was more common just a few decades ago. Broadly speaking, people want more meaning in their work and work with purpose. They want the work to fit who they are and not the other way around. They want to learn and grow, and to have multiple avenues for doing so. They may want to learn from online communities, from their peers, and from someone experienced in what they want to learn. They want to make their own decisions. Their … *our* … very identities are at stake! To adapt to this reality, people managers must become more highly skilled at engaging others. This story may provide a suitable example.

Upon graduating from college with a degree in International Relations in 1991, I was unsure of my career direction except knowing I wanted something "in international," to leverage my experiences abroad and foreign language skills in French, Spanish, and Russian. Without finding a good fit immediately and needing to be employed while thinking through options, I settled for a short-term administrative position at the State of Wisconsin Investment Board whose mission is to responsibly invest the retirement funds of state employees. In that role, I reported to two leaders, one of whom was John Nelson, a highly respected Portfolio Manager of Small-Cap Stocks and Investment Director. Every afternoon for the 7 months I worked in those offices, John would invite me to set aside my duties so I could observe his team meeting held just after market close. In this meeting, John and his team would gather and discuss market dynamics in their targeted industries, as well as their investment picks. In my case, I had absolutely no responsibilities besides listening for the length of the meeting, and then, I would go back to my regular responsibilities. As I think back on that time, I still recall feeling dumbfounded about John's choice to include me – wasn't he sacrificing company funds to involve someone who had no intention of staying in the organization or in the field of investing? Wasn't he concerned about my lower daily productivity and the cost the organization was paying? At the same time, I remember feeling pleased about the opportunity and was aware that he wanted me to learn something new. The love of investing did not ignite in me a new career direction, but I do remember watching very carefully how the team spoke to each other and how they interacted. (Go figure!) I also valued the chance to build relationships with each member of his team who were normally "heads down" in their offices behind computers and IPO prospectuses. In retrospect, I now see that this job was my introduction to a developmentally minded leader whose actions correspond to my definition above. Amazingly, John has reached out to me multiple times every year since then without fail to stay connected, has articulated many times the enjoyment he feels at watching my development and my career grow over time, and is still a coach and mentor to this day, 30 years later.

John inherently understood the importance of purpose and engaging employees. He invested in my personal growth and well-being, and offered what he could – exposure and access into a new world for a recent graduate. As he recently said to me, "You never know what will ignite a career passion." Interestingly, it was during that era that the topic of employee engagement had begun to be of keen interest to organizations, given the research emerging about the high costs of unmotivated workforces.[3]

Employee Engagement

The first researcher to suggest the strategic link between the effective management of people and positive business outcomes was a professor and scholar from Rutgers School of Management and Labor Relations in the field of organizational sciences, Mark Huselid. Starting in the 1990s, many stock-listed companies began to measure their intangible assets (i.e., people), based on predictions that the value of intangible assets would soon exceed that of tangible assets.[4] Huselid found that when managers became extensively involved in "high-performance work practices," their companies enjoyed higher motivation, less shirking of responsibility, higher retention of quality employees, and lower retention of non-performers. "Across a wide range of industries and firm sizes," Huselid says, "[I find] considerable support … that investments in such practices are associated with lower employee turnover and greater productivity and corporate financial performance."[5]

Today, the term "employee engagement" is the common term for Huselid's findings. In the Employee Engagement Survey from the Corporate Leadership Council's study, engagement is defined as the extent to which employees commit to something or someone in their organization, how hard they work, and how long they stay as a result of that commitment.[6] Measured by both quantitative measures (such as retention rates) and qualitative measures (discretionary effort), statistics show employees are less engaged than ever. In fact, a recent Gallup poll indicates that only 33% of U.S. employees consider themselves "engaged" at work versus 70% of the world's best organizations. Furthermore, 16% of employees report being disengaged – they are entirely unhappy in their jobs. The remaining 51% of employees are not engaged – they're just there.[7] In more bad news, 48% of workers leave their jobs because it wasn't what they expected it to be,[8] and when employees decide to leave, they don't seek to move to another part of the organization. Instead, they (91%) leave the company entirely.[9] Only about 20% of employees say they're managed in a way that motivates them to do great work.[10]

Globally, the picture is not necessarily better. In a separate study that delineates "fully engaged" as the top category (versus "partially engaged"), the United Arab Emirates has the highest percentage at 26%, while China has the lowest with just 6%. The USA sits snugly between the two at 17%. The study reveals that 84% of workers globally are just "coming to work" instead of contributing all they could as fully engaged employees.[11]

No matter that numbers vary between studies; the trend is horrific. What are organizations doing to create such a large group of unmotivated people? To be fair, the phenomenon of disengagement may start well before our careers do. William Edwards Deming, leader of the quality movement,[12] described our downward slide away from the virtues of childhood in this way:

> People are born with intrinsic motivation, self-esteem, dignity, curiosity to learn, joy in learning. [Unfortunately,] the forces of destruction begin with toddlers – a prize for the best Halloween costume, grades in school, gold stars, and up on through the university. On the job, people, teams, divisions are ranked – reward for those on the top, punishment for those on the bottom. MBO's, quotas, incentive pay, business plans, put together separately, division by division, cause further loss, unknown and unknowable.[13]

Developmental coaches seek to reverse that trend. When managers connect what's meaningful to the employee with what's needed in the business, they create the conditions for employees to fully engage.

Retention and Discretionary Effort

Lest we depress ourselves with the engagement statistics, there is opportunity in every challenge. When leaders learn the skills of engaging employees, the payoff is highly rewarding. In fact, this research is downright exciting and motivating. First, as mentioned, employee engagement is measured through two metrics: retention rates and discretionary effort.[14] Retention rates are a straightforward metric that go directly to the bottom line of any organization. Managers understand this cost, as it's often cited in the high cost of terminations, recruiting, and onboarding, not to mention productivity loss during employee transitions. In a global organization we know, an HR executive reported that her decision to stay in the company after a reorganization had easily saved the company $200,000, just counting the immediate hard costs.

The second metric used in measuring engagement is called "discretionary effort," which has a (top and bottom line) impact that managers can see and feel every single day. Discretionary effort refers to the extra effort that employees commit (or not) to a task that goes beyond the basic requirements, and evokes feelings of competence, contentedness, and belonging. "Discretionary," of course, is the key word because the effort that we're talking about is entirely optional and the choice of the employee. We're referring to the micro-choices that people make day after day, which when accompanied by feelings of engagement and motivation *result in an astounding 57% more discretionary effort and a 20% improvement of individual performance.*[15] Examples of discretionary effort include the choice to arrive at the office a little earlier (even 5-10 minutes), searching for an additional solution to a problem, deciding to recheck one's work for accuracy, taking time to specially thank someone for their help, devoting extra care to polish a presentation, or completing just a few more items before leaving for the day. (This corresponds to research that established that engaged employees take less sick leave, too.[16]) Zoom out from these statistics for a moment now and imagine the impact to your team and organization if everyone around you were happily willing to improve their performance by 20% every day! Similarly, the Corporate Leadership Council found that 71% of companies with above-average employee commitment had greater one-year revenue growth relative to their industry peer group than those with below-average employee commitment.[17] Knowing this fact should be a wake-up call for the aspiring manager-coach.

Stabilizing Forces in Times of Disruption

A complementary rational for developmental coaching lies in a wider perspective – the rapidly changing, global business context. The ongoing technology and market disruptions, not to mention the COVID-19 pandemic occurring at the time of this writing, creates for many a new kind of anxiety not felt or seen before in our lifetimes. These shifts, with their velocity, frequency, and complexity, force a "eat-or-get-eaten" mindset, prompting organizations to act and react as boldly as they are able. Even before the pandemic, 72% of organizations were currently pursuing some organizational change or transformation, all of which is highly destabilizing to employees and creates significant fear in the labor market.[18]

It's easy to see how anxiety is building with regard to the effort required and ability to keep up. More and more, managers with the skills to engage with – and on the topic of – emotion will be a stabilizing force for their organizations. Klaus Schwab, head of the World Economic Forum, points out that organizations must help fearful employees prepare for the future, or bear the possibility that labor markets be highly disruptive in the future. He insists, "I am convinced of one thing – that in the future it will be talent, more than capital, that will represent the critical factor of production."[19]

I remember well "Mari," a highly competent, junior member of the leadership team I was coaching. She was "junior" in that she reported to a member of the leadership team, but was included in each meeting nonetheless given her impressive analytical and project management skills. In general, she had a modest nature and was hesitant to speak up. One day, Mari walked into my "guest office" for our monthly, face-to-face coaching session, and asked if she could share something. She proceeded to read a list – a very long list – of her concerns about her job and role, including why this made her unhappy. It was plain that this was a catharsis of sorts, a plea for help. My reaction was surprise, then concern and empathy. I began with the basics, asking what kind of basic, emotional support she currently had. When she looked blankly, I inquired whether her spouse was able to be there for her, at which point she began to cry. She confirmed, as well, the deficit of sufficient support at home.

This was not a case of lack of engagement; Mari worked diligently and was a high performer. But her list harkened Schwab's warning to leaders: Managers must support employees to cope and prepare for the future. Importantly, her long list of concerns suggested numerous larger forces at play, which were coming at her fast and furious. For each employee, managers need to be able to spot fears and stressors to productively engage the person on these topics. Without a manager who can help work with the emotional landscape for each employee, the workplace will be more destabilizing than it needs to be.

Learning and Psychological Flexibility

It may seem we've left the obvious to last: developmental coaching accelerates learning. One could argue that people are already learning all the time, every day. But suggesting that people apply their incremental learning from one day to the next (this can also be called life experience) is reactive in nature: A mistake was made, and learning follows. Psychological flexibility, on the other hand, requires a more proactive stance, intentionally learning and unlearning over and over again.

In his book, *21 Lessons for the 21st Century* (2018), Yuval Harari, Israeli historian, philosopher, and professor, discusses the importance of psychological flexibility. "To survive and flourish … you will need a lot of mental flexibility and great reserves of emotional balance," and "You can't afford stability. If you try to hold on to some stable identity, job or worldview you risk being left behind as the world flies by you with a whoosh."[20]

Manager-coaches must provide ongoing challenge and support for people to go well beyond the status quo: Do more with less, meet ever-higher stakeholders' expectations, adapt to new technologies, incubate relevant innovations, assimilate new generations in the workforce, update or rebrand their value proposition, and reorganize when necessary – all while performing at higher levels than ever before. None of this is possible or sustainable unless managers and organizations are proficient at establishing ongoing practices which recognize, reward, and hold people accountable for being proactive about becoming more flexible thinkers. Developmental coaches don't get hooked by simple business-oriented problem-solving. They know the longer-term payoff of making learning acumen as a primary outcome of the working relationship.

Let's return to the case about Olivia, who you read about in the Introduction. In this version, we've provided Olivia more insights into what successful developmental coaching looks like.

Olivia's Case Study: A Promising Coaching Session

"Henry" is a talented and hard-working project manager in an engineering-manufacturing firm who finds himself increasingly frustrated because, despite his efforts, his team is not completing their deliverables on time. The missed deadlines are affecting the team's morale, as well as Henry's confidence in his own abilities as a leader. He's begun to work extremely long hours and finds himself spending extra time redoing the work his team members hurriedly submit. Henry's energy is waning. He wonders where all this will end up, because there are only so many hours in a day. (So far this is the same scenario as in the Introduction; from here, you'll notice differences.)

Olivia is Henry's manager. Olivia is also feeling increased pressure in her role due to Henry's team's financial results. She is getting pressure to "coach Henry." Olivia knows that she is ultimately responsible for the project's overall results as well as Henry's development, and as such, thinks of herself not just as a "manager" but as a "manager-coach." Olivia recognizes the opportunity for Henry to learn something new. Simultaneously, she recognizes her own chance to practice her coaching skills. She schedules a 50-minute meeting with Henry.

On the day of the meeting, Olivia spends time connecting with Henry personally and then transitions to the topic of the late deliverables and Henry's part in it as the team leader. Olivia provides her observations about what she's noticed about his hands-on approach with the team members, which he acknowledges. She asks him to relay examples that come to mind and develop an updated theory about what is underneath it. In doing so, Henry realizes that when under pressure, he micro-manages and exhausts himself. What's worse, his team is increasingly demotivated and the metrics are not improving. Henry develops a theory about himself: When he feels stress mounting, he fears the team won't step up willingly. To mitigate his anxiety, he proactively becomes more directive – telling others what to do. The team members mostly comply, but are slow to react and communicate, avoiding more directives. Together, Olivia and Henry identify what he most wants – to be able to remain open and collaborative when stressed while at the same time finding new ways to support himself and the team when the pressure is on. Olivia asks him to identify specifically how he'd personally benefit from doing so. Henry sees it clearly: he wants to become more resilient and less reactive. He wants to keep his emotions in check and find new ways of supporting himself and his team. They discuss all points in detail. Olivia agrees and they identify a more scoped, developmental topic for today's discussion: How Henry can slow himself down and catch himself from over-reacting when under pressure. When Olivia asks how she can be most useful in the conversation, Henry asks Olivia to listen to him talk it through and to react to his ideas. With Olivia's prompts, Henry then ponders his current ideas aloud, all but one which sound very constructive to Olivia. She points out her one concern but notes that the decision is ultimately Henry's. Olivia encourages him to identify several experiments to test his ideas about slowing things down when under pressure which he does. Olivia shares her own strategy for staying calm under pressure to further stimulate his thinking. They close with several questions from Olivia about how Henry feels about the conversation and next steps.

Because Henry feels supported by Olivia throughout the conversation, the relationship does not suffer even though Olivia gave him some difficult feedback early in the conversation. In fact, Henry feels that the trust with her is stronger than before. His enthusiasm increases, and he is ready to get back to work with a new perspective.

Olivia's confidence has increased, too. She's used a coaching skillset and mindset to support Henry differently, resulting in Henry leaving upbeat and engaged. This successful coaching experience – and subsequent growth and development of the coachee – is facilitated by the coach's ability to track four major elements at the same time:

1. The path and overall direction of the developmental conversation with its three phases.
2. The level of engagement on the topic of development which pertains to the resolving of the business issue being discussed.
3. The emotional experience of the coachee, resulting in a heightened (or at least not diminished) level of trust with the coach.
4. The coach's own feelings and observations, selectively sharing with the coachee in support of the objectives.

In the next chapter, we'll begin our study of the Developmental Coaching Model (DCM) and identify the elements of what made Olivia's coaching more effective this time, so that you can apply them yourself.

Notes

1 "He" of "one" added by author.

2 Retrieved from: https://coachfederation.org/about.

3 Sibbet, D. (1997). 75 years of management ideas and practice 1922–1997. *Harvard Business Review*, 75(5), 2-12.

4 KPMG (2010). Intangible assets and goodwill in the context of business combinations. Retrieved from: https://www.consultancy.nl/media/KPMG%20-%20 Intangible%20Assets%20and%20Goodwill-836.pdf.

5 Huselid used diverse measures of performance and adjusted for biases in the study. His estimates implied both a constant level of investment each year in these practices and implied an increasing use of these practices. Huselid, M. A. (1995). The impact of human resource management practices on turnover, productivity, and corporate financial performance. *Academy of Management Journal, 38*(3), 635-672.

6 Employee Engagement Survey from the Corporate Leadership Council (2004).

7 Gallup developed State of the American Workplace using data collected from more than 195,600 U.S. employees via the Gallup Panel and Gallup Daily tracking in 2015 and 2016, and more than 31 million respondents through Gallup's Q12 Client Database. Gallup (2017). *State of the American Workplace.*

8 Bolden-Barrett, V. (2019, March 27) Study: 48% of workers have left a job because it didn't meet expectations. Retrieved from: https://www.hrdive.com/news/ study-48-of-workers-have-left-a-job-because-it-didnt-meet-expectations/551179/.

9 O'Boyle, E., and Mann, A. (2017, May 15). American workplace changing at a dizzying pace. Retrieved from https://www.gallup.com/workplace/236282/ american-workplace-changing-dizzying-pace.aspx.

10 Gallup (2017). *State of the American Workplace.*

11 ADP Research Institute's 19-country Global Study of Engagement provides a global benchmark for engagement. The study surveyed more than 19,000 employees around the globe (one thousand per country in a stratified random sample to measure their level of engagement and identify the work conditions most likely to attract and retain talent.) For more information, see: ADP (2019, June 14). *ADP Research Institute Sets International Benchmark for Employee Engagement with its 19-Country Global Study of Engagement.* Retrieved from: https://www.prnewswire.com/news-releases/adp-research-institute-sets- international-benchmark-for-employee-engagement-with-its-19-country-global- study-of-engagement-300867645.html.

12 Deming was credited by the Japanese as helping the nation rise from the ashes in the 1950s and 1960s and become the second largest economy of the world after WWII, in particular for his contribution to the Japanese auto industry. For more, see Senge, P. M. (2006). *The Fifth Discipline: The Art and Practice of the Learning Organization.* New York, NY: Doubleday.

13 Drucker, P. F. (1974) *Management: Tasks, Responsibilities, Practices.* New York, NY: Harper and Row.

14 According to the 2008-2009 Corporate Leadership Council, five factors contributed to employee perception of a high "employee value proposition" (EVP), defined as the extent to which the labor market and employees perceive the value they gain by being employed by a particular organization. The EVP score was shown to drive performance, attraction (recruiting), commitment (discretionary effort), and retention (how long they stayed). While all of these elements are important, the commitment factor (discretionary effort) is of special interest because it links most directly to the concept of engagement.

15 Birdie, A. K. (2017). *Employees and Employers in Service Organizations: Emerging Challenges and Opportunities*. Waretown, NJ: Apple Academic Press.

16 Crabb, S. (2011). The use of coaching principles to foster employee engagement. *The Coaching Psychologist, 7*(1), 27-34.

17 According to the Corporate Leadership Council workforce study (2004), above average employee commitment is defined as having more than 11% of an organization's workforce fall into the highly committed category. Below average employee commitment is defined as having less than 11% of an organization's workforce fall into the highly committed category. For more, see: Driving employee performance and retention through employee engagement: A quantitative analysis of effective engagement strategies (2004). *Corporate Executive Board*. Retrieved from: https://www.academia.edu/15293625/ Driving_Performance_and_Retention_Through_Employee_Engagement.

18 Ibid.

19 Schwab, K. (2019). The fourth industrial revolution: What it means, how to respond. *World Economic Forum*. Retrieved from: https://www.weforum.org/ agenda/2016/01/the-fourth-industrial-revolution-what-it-means-and-how-to-respond/.

20 Harari, Y. N. (2018). *21 Lessons for the 21st Century*. New York, NY: Random House.

Chapter 2

The Developmental Coaching Model

There is nothing more practical than a good theory.

– Kurt Lewin

I began my professional career as a linguist. Languages open a new world of people, ideas, and ways of thinking and living, and, I love the idea of building relationships with other people that I otherwise couldn't. I lived abroad 7 times before I turned 30, but it all started in my eighth-grade French class.

If you've taken language classes many years ago, you may recall memorizing "dialogues." I still remember the first time we were assigned to recite one in its entirety, one-by-one in the back of the room, facing our French teacher:

(Maman)	« *Michel, Anne, vous travaillez?* »
(Les enfants)	« *Ah, non, nous regardons la télévision, pourquoi?* »
(Maman)	« *Les Duponts arrivent dans une heure!* »
(Les enfants)	« *S'il te plaît, maman, encore 5 minutes!* »
(Maman)	« *Pas question, il y a beaucoup à faire.* » (…)

I don't remember learning much from this way of teaching. It felt like memorizing a series of sounds, and even though I somehow remember the sentences today, I remember being highly dubious of its effectiveness at the time. In fact, there's a linguist joke that warns of the real problem here: No one knows the other half of the dialogue!

Memorizing a set of sentences – a dialogue – is a kind of model for how to learn something. In the same way, through this book, you'll be introduced to a model for how to learn coaching. A good model describes the landscape but can never include everything to be considered. Models highlight something needing emphasis from the perspective of the author: theory, methodology, structure, and/or principles. In the same way, the steps in this model will provide you many "dots" of information, which, when combined with your people management experience, will form a bigger "whole," a bigger *gestalt*. It will hopefully be more useful than memorizing dialogues.

The Developmental Coaching Model (DCM) incorporates adult development learning theory, including the crucible idea that people accept their own ideas much faster than they'll accept those of others. For sustainable change, people must be in the center of their own learning, because they ultimately reject being told what to do. This process model provides direction, enabling the manager-coach to effectively move from a business challenge to a developmental conversation while leveraging the experiences, talents, and ideas of the coachee. This is a critical change in what many employees expect today. Transforming the conversation while also putting the coachee in the driver's seat is the game-changing differentiator for individuals and organizations.[1]

Why *This* Model?

There are several reasons to create a new model when other models already exist. The priorities with this coaching model are to:

1. Resolve business issues while *at the same time* develop people. Sustainable business growth and restoring more caring workplaces require the *fusing* of what are typically two separate conversations.
2. Incorporate the topic of motivation explicitly into each conversation. Managers can learn what motivates their people which leads to sincere engagement and sustainable, rather than temporary, change.
3. Leverage the attributes of resistance as a natural, healthy, and important aspect of self-awareness, development, and change.
4. Provide a tool applicable in diverse, multicultural and global environments. Coaches need tools that illuminate the assumptions that drive beliefs and actions.

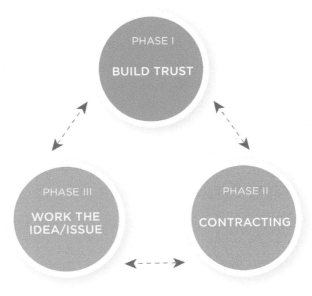

Figure 2.1   The Developmental Coaching Model: a high-level view.

A High-Level View of the Developmental Coaching Model (DCM)

Looking at the model from a high level, you'll see three phases: "Build Trust," "Contracting," and "Work the Idea/Issue." (Figure 2.1).

The high-level model helps the coach know where she is in the coaching process at any time should she lose her way. This view is like zooming out on your GPS to establish which cities you will visit on your road trip. Notice the arrows go both directions because returning to a prior city will be necessary if you drove by too quickly! Coaches learn that insufficient time with any given phase will result in the need to back up later.

The Developmental Coaching Model (DCM)

The full Developmental Coaching Model (DCM) is comprised of seven steps, as seen in Figure 2.2. Notice how many steps per phase.

Phase I – Build Trust (Step #1)

Phase I is comprised of only one step: "Establish a Climate of Trust." Of course, in life, trust is neither a step, nor a phase. It's more of an outcome of past experience and the current moment, which becomes woven into the fabric of the relationship itself. For this reason, most coaching models place trust as a backdrop. The DCM, however, brings trust to the fore as a reminder that manager-coaches must earn an *adequate* trust before attempting to coach, and then consider what is needed in the moment to ensure an ongoing environment of safety and openness.

Phase II – Contracting (Steps #2, #3, and #4)

The goal of Phase II is to reach an agreement – or, a "psychological contract" – to define a *developmental topic*, and *why* and *how. It's this series of explicit agreements that make coaching distinct from other types of workplace communication.* In Step #2, the coach and coachee together answer the questions: "What is the topic and what is the developmental dilemma it represents?"; "why is it important?"; and "what would achieving this bring you/do for you?" All this may be derived from a need, opportunity, or concern about the person in relation to their role or in the business. In Step #3, the scope of the topic is right-sized for the moment: which part of the developmental topic does the coachee want to address in this moment? Then, if an agreement on the topic can be established, the coachee moves to Step #4 and "how the coach can be most useful (in this coaching conversation)."
In this step, the coach asks the client to be clear about what support is actually needed (explore different ideas? play devil's advocate? role-play?). Asking the question signals to the coachee that he's in charge of his own learning, as well as helps him determine what specific support is truly needed.

If the coach finds herself at any time pushing or cajoling the coachee to take on the topic, she knows the coachee is not ready to move to Phase III. The arrow pointing away from the cycle at Step #3 represents what happens psychologically and/or emotionally when the coach and coachee have not reached an agreement, and have exited the coaching process. The conversation may continue, but it won't be coaching. The coach will need to determine which prior step was not fully established and what precluded it: Does the coachee need more information? Did the coachee not see the importance or benefit of addressing the topic? In some cases, backing up to Step #1 will be required, because the trust is insufficient.

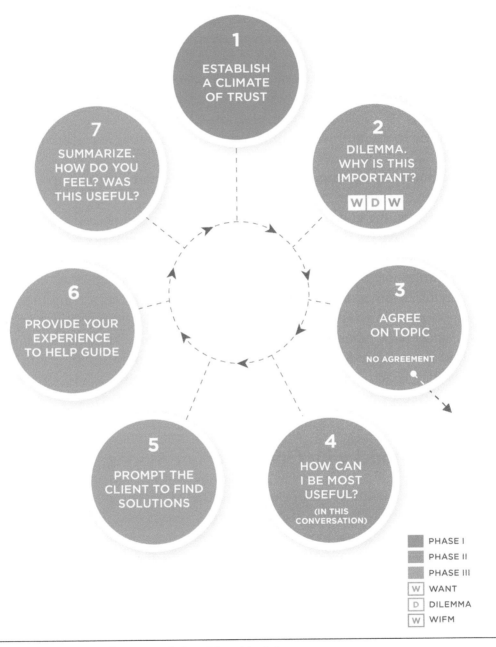

Figure 2.2 The Developmental Coaching Model.

Phase III – Work the Idea/Issue (Steps #5, #6, #7)

You might think of the last three steps of the model as the actioning part of the coaching, because together the coach and coachee go deeper into the agreed-upon topic in the agreed-upon way. In Step #5, the coach prompts the coachee for ideas and they explore together. In Step #6, the coach may choose to share a reaction, supportive statement, push the conversation deeper, or expand the thinking, but avoids taking over or acting as the arbiter of right and wrong. If the coachee has generated a satisfying set of ideas in Step #5, the coach may not need to give any further comment, in effect, skipping Step #6. Closing the conversation with Step #7 is the final step and the time to identify what's next, reinforce what was learned, and share reflections about the conversation.

The detailed model suggests an orderly, sequential approach to the conversation, but reality intervenes – clients may back up or say something which confuses the coach. But know that the client cannot be faulted for not following the coach's path! (As mentioned, the client will not have memorized the other half of the dialogue!) The coach's challenge, therefore, is to do two things: use the model to guide the conversation, while at the same time staying firmly in the present by listening intently and staying mentally and emotionally with the coachee. As necessary, the coach gently brings the conversation back when the conversation wanders too far afield. Coaches may find it beneficial to keep a copy of the model physically in front of them as they coach until the steps come naturally. Doing so makes it easier to react and respond to what is being said and felt.

Using the Model with One's Peers or Manager

For reasons of hierarchy and power (and the expectations and assumptions that accompany), coaching a direct report is considered more straightforward than coaching one's peers or manager. After all, the role of a people manager is to help develop her team (and this is also the direct report's expectation). That said, coaching peers or managers is very much in reach for coaches with adequate skills and an amenable context. Differences in approach are found primarily in how the coach works through the Contracting phase. For details on what to consider, see Chapter 4.

It's Practice that Matters

Returning to the analogy from French class, need I mention that learning vocabulary and grammar rules do not equate to being fluent? After four years of language instruction before moving to France at age 16, I vividly remember instances of discomfort and distress when presented with a question that I couldn't yet handle. (One, in particular, stays with me: "Tu t'en vas?" Xavier had asked me. At that point, I had only learned the translation of "Are you leaving now?" but not yet the more colloquial "Taking off?") I'd ask myself later "How hadn't I learned that yet?" Over time, I'd be more gentle with myself, reminding myself that if it were easy to learn it all quickly, everyone would be multilingual. The same goes for coaching. Reading about coaching is mostly an intellectual exercise and the ideas in these pages will remain here – not integrated into your leadership repertoire – without the willingness and dedication to practice. Our coaching workshop, for example, would undoubtedly increase your confidence and propel you forward as a manager-coach because of the emphasis on practice. But this is a book.

So consider, then, treating this book as a foundational primer that leads to a series of experiments. For each concept that grabs your attention, stop reading and try it. As you notice the result of each experiment, you'll be gathering data to refine your approach, readying yourself to try again. Some experiments will not go the way you hoped, but that's the nature of experimentation – to learn from what happened. So take the pressure off from being an excellent coach immediately. Says one of the most respected authors in the field of leadership, Warren Bennis, focus on "doing the right things" more than "doing things right."[2] By learning as you go and not expecting perfection, you continue your own path of discovery.

Let's get started.

Notes

1 Schein, E. H. (2010). *Organizational Culture and Leadership* (5th Ed.). Hoboken, NJ: John Wiley & Sons.
2 Bennis, W. G., & Townsend, R. (1989). *On Becoming a Leader* (Vol. 36). Reading, MA: Addison-Wesley.

Chapter 3

Phase I: Build Trust

Connection: the energy that exists between people when they feel seen, heard, and valued; when they can give and receive without judgment; and when they derive substance and strength from the relationship.

— Brené Brown

If you've ever wondered how important relationships and trust *really* are in getting results, consider the story reported in *The New York Times* of a professional DJ named Azmyth Kaminski who agreed to cut off his dreadlocks and present himself as a financial planner to potential clients.[1] The goal of the exercise designed by the Certified Financial Planner Board of Standards was to see how people screen a financial planner and to what extent the general public could determine competence in money managers. Mr. Kaminski was great with people and was able to build rapport quickly with others. So, he learned a few key financial words and then allowed himself to be interviewed in a conference room for 15 minutes to a series of potential clients. The result? In all but one case, Mr. Kaminski was hired for the job, proof that the power of rapport and the ability to build trust quickly is not to be underestimated. Even after the individuals found out the true identity of the imposter, there was still one who said he didn't mind and wanted Mr. Kaminski to manage his money regardless!

No one, including you, wants to have a money manager – or a coach – who is untrusted. The relationship itself evokes fear and feelings of vulnerability because when a person who we hold in authority discusses our future, along with the power to give or take away, how much more sensitive can it really get? Broadly speaking, how a coach engages should instill a sense of safety: How the manager holds conversations, deals with learning opportunities, and navigates awkward situations. The coach is demonstrating that others can count on her no matter what. This is why "Establish a Climate of Trust" is Step 1 of the coaching model (See Figure 2.2).

Want to Get Better at Trust?

Like Mr. Kaminski, some people are very good at establishing trust. For others, it won't be so natural or happen so quickly. But to be clear: Trust-building is not something that only *some* are capable of – it's a skillset you can learn to get better at, establishing it more effectively and quickly. Your ability to trust – and be trustworthy – can be significantly improved with the motivation to understand the key principles and apply what you learn.

For some reason, however, managers often seem ambivalent on whether taking time to build trust falls into the "nice-to-have" or "must-have" category. We can all point to examples of how trust meant the difference between enormous success and abject failure, but we still don't fully commit to working on trust as an object of focus. Perhaps this is because we never know if the time spent will really pay off, or how long it will take to achieve. Perhaps we believe that achieving trust is stubbornly dependent on how long you've known a person or use the "let's wait and see" approach. There are also the stances of "trust but verify" and the "trust just takes time." It's as if we're noncommittal or dubious until, magically, we realize: "Yes, I *do* trust you."

Interestingly, we don't seem to ponder the consequences of *low* trust. Low trust creates a drag in relationships and slows down every decision. In his book, *The Speed of Trust*, Steven M. R. Covey correlates low trust as a tax imposed on every relationship.[2] When considered this way, we stop thinking about trust as *taking* our time and instead see building it as an investment that *gives us back* time. In the preface of the book, Covey likens trust to an aquifer, a

> huge pool under the earth that feeds all the subsurface wells. In business and life, these wells are often called innovation, complementary teams, collaboration, empowerment … brand loyalty, or other strategic initiatives. These wells themselves feed the rivers and streams of human interaction, business commerce, and deal

making. They give sustaining quality of life to all relationships, including family relationships, interdepartmental relationships, day-to-day supplier and customer relationships – in fact, any effort – to make a sustainable contribution.[3]

Covey (2006, p. xxvi)

The topic of trust is vast. Amazon produces 100,000+ resources when typing "trust" into the search bar. Perhaps more important than establishing the value of it is to consider the rate at which it develops: How can we *accelerate the process*? The aim of this chapter, then, is to identify the accelerators in the context of coaching and explore related challenges. Let's begin by acknowledging some of the complexities and look at two trust rules.

Can We Really Expect to Adequately Understand Trust?

The topic of trust is complex because we humans are, well, complex. Life experiences will dictate how much one trusts, how much one is trusted, and under which circumstances. It comes fairly easily with some and very slowly with others. Nobody's wrong or bad; it's just that one's point of reference is impacted by many things – our sense of identity, individual psychology, family experience, geography of upbringing, cultural context, and so on. As an example, one person I know very well has such a positive attitude all the time; I can't seem to fully trust him. For me, knowing the other end of his emotional spectrum would help me be convinced of his optimism. I have felt unsure, for example, if he would deliver bad news to me or let me know if I had offended him. My lack of clarity about what causes him unease inhibits a sense of growth in my relationship.

As another example, my father has a big heart but doesn't trust much in anyone – especially someone who tries to sell him something. Recently, I asked him how he liked the no-cost, men's conference he attended on the topic of happiness. He had enjoyed the conference overall until he suddenly soured on the whole thing because at the end the speaker revealed he was selling financial management services. "But Dad," I said, "you've been looking for a financial planner anyway. If you liked him, maybe you should call him?" No matter, my father will not be sold to. Nor will he respond favorably to anyone he perceives as pushing a strong point of view. At work, he never trusted anyone in management.

Even if we could get beyond our individual proclivities on the topic, the complexity thickens for those who work remotely, across geographies or time zones. How is trust built with differences in mother tongues and with those who hold fundamentally different assumptions and sensibilities? For example, when approaching the coaching topic of motivation, a common, goal-oriented, Western question might be "What do you want to do in the future?" or "What are your goals for yourself long-term?" These questions sound simple and straightforward, but others will find them inextricably tied to family, responsibilities, and relationships. The coachee may feel blocked in responding because embedded in the question is the notion of individual aspiration which doesn't correspond to their own values. Trust then stagnates because the coachee feels culturally disconnected. A more suitable question might be "What is your greatest hope for your family?"; "What is your family's greatest hope for you?"; "What is your greatest hope for your own future?"; "How might you work through any differences to find a solution that is acceptable for both your family and you?" With this as just one of many cultural nuances, how does a remote manager become sensitized without extensive time in that region?

I once had the opportunity to coach a Chinese Singaporean who had different points of reference about development. It was difficult for him to have any coach provided to him from his company, he said, because in his culture the "student" must discover his own "teacher" – two of his former managers continue as his teachers to this day. My own point of reference is very different: I have several, decades-long trusted coaches ("teachers"), but also enjoy numerous people who support me in different ways. I would welcome a dedicated coach through my employer because I appreciate the experience of tapping into different people with unique perspectives, and expect trust can develop.

With so many concepts of trust-building, coaches might assume there's no use in really trying to build it. And yet, there are universal principles and practices that apply. One is that building trust more quickly requires exquisite listening skills and engaging with people's interiors. We still find managers, however, who are famous for their inability to listen or who still point to the outdated wisdom of keeping emotions out of the workplace, which has been rethought decades ago in the literature on motivation. This is not to say that all *coachees* are able and willing to share their interiors when they are speaking with their manager, but a skilled manager-coach who can access their own emotions can often make it possible. This is also not to say that managers who declare emotions as off-limits for any reason *cannot* be successful, but it's likely their employees must seek their support on emotionally sensitive topics elsewhere. As such, these same managers are operating without as much information and are not seeing what could be possible if they were to broaden their repertoire.

The need for meaningful exchanges becomes more and more relevant given the increasing stressors in our workplaces. As employees face constant change, they are continually being asked to let go of what has come before – perhaps the most difficult of human processes – and absorb what is new. Since psychological and emotional processing lags well behind each change event, employees can get "stuck" without the chance to externalize or process that change.[4] For example, imagine you learned this week that a favorite product or service to which you've dedicated years of your life will soon be discontinued. While you intellectually understand, the psychological and emotional processing of the fact can take weeks or months, siphoning away energy from otherwise productive work time. The ability and interest of your manager-coach, however, to engage about the change and what it means to you would speed the process of adaptation. Creating time and space for meaningful topics in our fast-paced workplaces of today is an important practice. As we'll see, the extent to which a coach can support the coachee to connect workplace challenges to his wants and needs is predicated on the ability to gain and maintain sufficient trust.

Two Rules of Trust

With the coaching context in mind, I like the simplicity of the following two rules of trust as a starting place. Trust results from a belief that the other (1) has your best interest at heart and (2) is competent in a way that corresponds to the situation.

Take the case of a European coaching client of mine, "Stéphane," a highly respected financial services executive who was well known for his ability to manage more clients and drive higher margins than any of his colleagues. He relayed to me that his manager, "John" – fairly new in the role and new to Stéphane – had requested a conversation with him on a recent Monday morning. Stéphane knew there was a team issue of some kind to discuss, and that an employee was upset with him and had complained to HR. John opened the conversation in a casual manner, asking Stéphane what he did over the weekend, presumably to create ease and openness for a fruitful conversation. Stéphane responded that he and his wife had spent the weekend outdoors, hiking for an entire day and then running a 10-mile trail together on the following day. John jumped on the information quickly, making the weekend's activities a bridge to his topic for the day: That working with Stéphane is like running a marathon and that he pushes people too hard and never gives them a break. The message was delivered for over an hour, with Stéphane working to hold back his anger and the feeling of being personally attacked. His manager told him he'd need to categorically change the way he was leading and delegating work if he wanted to be successful at the firm, in particular that he should emulate a sprinter, not a marathoner, and to distribute more work to those who could handle it versus distribute it evenly. In the end, Stéphane stated his disagreement with all points and the meeting ended abruptly. Stéphane was angry and frustrated.

Rule #1: Have the Coachee's Best Interest at Heart

The first rule of trust is having the coachee's best interest at heart. From the outside, I could argue that Stéphane's manager did have Stéphane's best interest at heart. My data is that John had spent over an hour with him and provided specific suggestions to help Stéphane see his blind spots. Unfortunately, what was less clear is whether John was focused on solving a problem or supporting a person. From Stéphane's perspective, he had shared details of his private life only to have his manager use them to launch an attack. Stéphane interpreted his manager's actions as mean-spirited and even "vindictive," imagining that his manager had taken some pleasure in finally finding something to "get on him" due to jealousy about his years of impressive results. Energy and endurance are part of Stéphane's identity and success, and he had been rewarded for it along the way. Now Stéphane felt blamed in what he perceived was a rare misstep. Although John may have had good intentions, Stéphane would not be coached by him. To achieve the first criterion of trust, he'll need to integrate different behaviors and for Stéphane to experience his support in more satisfying ways.

Rule #2: Be Contextually Competent

The second criterion is being competent in a way that corresponds to the situation. As an example, I don't necessarily trust a brain surgeon to know time management or business acumen, but will trust her insights on topics relevant to her expertise. In the situation with Stéphane, John needs competency in both coaching and effective ways to give feedback. Interestingly, Stéphane admitted to me that he was interested in the idea of sprints versus marathons and wanted to discuss it. It's unfortunate that John will not be a coach or resource to Stéphane until achieving criterion #1.

How to Accelerate Trust

> The wisdom begins in wonder.
>
> **— Socrates**

To consider the breadth and diversity of factors that contribute to building trust could overrun this book, but getting the fundamentals right provides a much greater chance of getting lucky.[5] Here are seven fundamentals to accelerate trust. In no particular order, these happen simultaneously and overlap.

Increase Curiosity

People want relationships and trust to come naturally and quickly, but in practice, they often develop very slowly. One way to accelerate trust is through the simple, but powerful, practice of being more curious. Curiosity is the "desire for new information that results in exploration and new knowledge."[6] Most people think they are already curious, but with important caveats. First, some have lots of questions, but don't actually ask. Others ask aloud, but only to confirm what they already know or expect to hear. Others ask questions but don't care to hear the answers. In the prior scenario with Stéphane, for example, the curiosity seemed to be about solving the issue, not about Stéphane. It's unclear, for example, whether John was curious about Stéphane's view of the situation, the challenges he faces as a leader, his goals for the project, how he felt when hearing about the complaint, and so on. To increase trust, curiosity about *the person* matters – a lot.

Curiosity is sometimes understood as polite questioning. Asking about someone's kids when you're not really interested will result in a conversation you have little energy for. Trust is not being built. Instead, ask yourself what *does* interest you when you consider this person? Is it his style, work ethic, philosophy to life, ability to influence others, perspective on a particular topic, background? What do you really want to know? If you feel blocked or cannot find a topic, stimulate your curiosity by spending more time noticing: What's on the person's desk? What does she talk about in the interstitial moments? What does she seem to value most about herself? Does her LinkedIn profile highlight an interest? Then, ask about what truly captured your attention. (If you still can't find anything to ask, then get curious about that!)

CURIOSITY PROMPTS

- Write down everything you know (or think you know) about the person. What questions emerge?

- Be curious and authentic. Only ask what truly interests you.

- If you have trouble identifying what authentically interests you, spend more time observing.

- As you listen, focus on absorbing and learning.

WHICH ASPECTS OF YOUR ROLE ARE MOST MEANINGFUL TO YOU? WHY?

I'D LIKE TO UNDERSTAND … ABOUT YOU.

WHAT BROUGHT YOU TO THIS PROFESSION / JOB / COMPANY?

I'M CURIOUS (WONDER) ABOUT…

WHAT'S THE BIGGEST PERSONAL CHALLENGE YOU FACE IN YOUR ROLE?

I NOTICE…

WHAT'S HAPPENING IN YOUR FIELD THAT'S INTERESTING TO YOU?

It can be harder to generate curiosity with those who are very different from you. Research reveals that "smaller knowledge gaps will arouse more curiosity and stimulate more exploratory behavior than having perceptions of...larger knowledge gaps."[7] The perception of smaller knowledge gaps produce a psychological "tension" to complete one's understanding. For example, if I meet someone from a country where I've lived, a desire to ask questions and close the perceived, smaller knowledge gap is easily evoked.

In other cases, I may need to work harder to become more curious. I remember one such an experience involving "Raymond," a global operations director and client who I struggled to trust. Raymond was the economic buyer, but my work was with his direct report and team. Our interactions were limited to bi-weekly check-ins, but I noticed how persistently critical Raymond was of the team, and at some point I determined he was generally an unkind person. At the same time, I could see that my lack of trust in his positive intent could mean this project would not end well. I needed to rethink my assumptions by heightening my curiosity dramatically. So, I began an exercise to answer the question "What do I want to know or understand about Raymond?" I ended with a page worth of judgmental questions, and nothing I could ever really ask, but by the time I got to page two and three, a number of questions reflected both non-judgment *and* authentic curiosity. Using those curiosities in my subsequent conversations resulted in a palpable increase in my empathy and, importantly, heightened trust in him as a person. While Raymond and I never became kindred spirits, I believe this effort allowed us to find the necessary common ground we needed to be satisfied with the relationship alongside the project.

Never Stop Raising Your Self-Awareness

Self-awareness is a tricky topic: Ask your team to raise their hand if they believe themselves to be self-aware, and every hand goes up. In reality, we're all self-aware to some extent, but how many blind spots do we have, and compared to whom? It's like the statistics on how people rate their own driving: Each of us is above average.

I remember the day encountering one of my blind spots. I was driving to see a client at a manufacturing plant in Nogales, Mexico, along with a supply chain consultant, "Fred," who frequently worked at the site on the same days. Central to the story is the fact that I'm a petite woman with shoulder-length hair and Fred was an average-sized, balding man. Over the course of a year, Fred and I developed a good amount of trust, and one day we began to compare observations and share what we were learning. That day, I commented on the lack of women at higher levels in the company and the fact that over the last year, I noticed all those promoted were physically big men. I gave examples. There was silence from Fred. He was looking out the window thoughtfully and I awaited his comment, imagining it would be about gender and bias, or perhaps promotions. Then, very serious and deep in thought, he said, "You know, that's very interesting. What I've noticed is that there are no balding men." I couldn't stop myself from a burst of laughter, recognizing that a small-framed female and a balding man would have the observations we did. From the Babylonian Talmud: "We don't see things as they are, we see them as we are."

If we can notice and accept the fact that our own perceptions are always different from those of others, we're able to develop humility about what we don't know or can't see. An ongoing recognition of our blind spots also gives us empathy for others with theirs.

Perhaps the best way to raise awareness of blind spots is to habitually ask for feedback. 360-degree assessment tools gather data from people who sit, metaphorically, 360 degrees around a person (typically direct reports, peers, and a manager, at a minimum). These are often done survey-style or through live interviews. But feedback can also be gathered every day by inviting others to react to your comments, expressing their feelings, or encourage questions and challenging ideas. It's being open to learn from others each day which builds self-awareness and trust.

Stay in the Present

Among the most difficult of practices while coaching is that of staying fully present to what is happening right in front of us (and within us). Committing to being in the present means training your brain to stay with what is happening now (and how we feel about what is happening now). Being aware allows a person to use data from the current moment (internally or externally) to inform a choice or next step, which impacts the future. Change only happens in the present moment, so noticing matters.

A number of years ago I stopped by the office of the Director of Finance, "Hugo," and saw he was typing. He looked up, smiled, and began to chat with me, but continued to move his fingers quickly on the keyboard as we spoke. Hugo never looked away from me, but also never stopped typing. As I expressed my surprise, he proudly confirmed that yes, he was used to talking to people as he typed, and that he had a unique ability to do both tasks perfectly well! Without exactly wanting to, I let out a laugh because of the impossibility of doing both 100% effectively. Hugo is not superhuman, and the research regarding multi-tasking is well-established. What I was curious about was the impact he was having on others. How many colleagues had cut the conversation short when they saw he was not affording his full attention? People expect others to be fully present; anything less can erode trust instead of build it.

Tips to Stay in the Present

- Meet in a private space where you will not be interrupted.
- If you are not in a suitable location or appropriate moment to have a discussion, look for a better place or moment. Move away from your desk and all visual distractions.
- Establish ahead of time how much time is available and what you propose if you run out of time, so your brain doesn't wander to the past or future. If your brain does wander, address it, so you can come back to the present. For example, "I'm distracted by the fact I don't know when my next appointment is. Do you mind if I quickly check so I can better focus?"
- Instead of being concerned you'll forget what your coachee is saying, take notes. Whether your notes are in relation to the conversation or to put ideas about unrelated topics out of your mind, notes are a great way to stay focused on what the coachee is saying. And *do* mention to the coachee why you are writing so they are not distracted. Remember that watching a manager take notes as she talks could cause concern, so be sure to explain what you will do with those notes.

"Join" Others

"Joining" refers to the multiple ways that humans establish commonality with one another. It's a useful skill to soothe the physiological reactions that come with stress. Joining with others can be as simple as sharing an appreciation, mirroring the other's communication style, pointing out what you agree with, or reciprocating similar energy: If you notice excitement, celebration, seriousness, or concern, bring forth the same energy to match it.

"Joining" counteracts the work of our ancient limbic system, the brain's mechanism meant to alert us to attacks and threats to survival. Today, even minor stressors we face at work can produce impulses to fight or run because our limbic systems have not yet evolved to recognize that modern-day stressors do not necessitate catecholamine hormones, such as adrenaline, that were needed when being chased by a tyrannosaurus rex in the Mesozoic era. If we agree in *one* way, the nervous system reasons, maybe we'll be alike in *other* ways, too. The nervous system can de-charge or relax.

What are your skills and resources to enable ease and joining as you talk with others? My partner, for example, invited his staff for weekly "walk-and-talks" with his dog, Mocha Bean. Imagine yourself there…your manager walking next to you (in contrast to across a table) and discussing a topic of mutual interest along with a happy Australian shepherd prancing ahead in the expansive outdoors on a crisp autumn day. It's hard to see how the environment would not support a positive outcome. Per the example, joining is represented not just in the words spoken but also in the physical experience of being in partnership. At a minimum, avoid creating an experience of (somatically) being in opposition to someone. In an office environment, for example, place chairs side-by-side, or around the corner of a table, instead of sitting knee to knee or (worse) on opposite sides of a table or desk. Other examples of joining:

■ Sitting in a similar position as the client
■ Adapting to the energy of the client – e.g., being excited when they are or being subdued when they are.
■ "I know we are both very busy, so thank you for making time for this conversation." Very sincere "thanking" potentially matches two individual's intentions of wanting to collaborate.
■ "Your development is one of my top priorities as a people manager and I know development is important to you, also." Acknowledging a common goal brings a sense of partnership.

Joining is not just for the opening sentences. As the conversation evolves, returning to trust using joining solidifies the groundwork for examining differences:

■ "I'm glad you've brought up this difficult topic. I appreciate it. This is a very good opportunity for us to work through it together."
■ "Please keep explaining; this is important."
■ Joining is not meant to indicate the need to agree. A good rule of thumb is that the more difficult the conversation is (and the more tentative the trust), the more often the coach should seek to join in different ways. Finding something to appreciate is easier for some than others, but in all cases ensure your comments are authentic.

Detect Non-Verbal Language and Context

In coaching, there is a lot of information zipping back and forth, most of it subtle and hard to name in the moment; it's an embodied experience. If you want to know how someone feels about what you are saying, remember that body language accounts for approximately 55% of the speaker's message. Tone of voice constitutes around 38%. The remaining 7% are the words actually spoken. While this is not true of someone explaining a profit and loss report or reciting facts and figures, it applies when the speaker is describing his/her attitude or point of view.[8]

A colleague of mine is 6 feet, 6 inches., a full 14 inches. taller than me. He is aware that his size, gender, and deep voice have an impact on others, possibly evoking a feeling of intimidation or domination. Without him saying or doing anything, his presence communicates "I'm in charge." So he consciously sits and stands in a compact way and monitors the volume of his voice. I, on the other hand, may choose to bring more of myself forward in those same situations, given that my physical size, voice, and gender may result in my contribution being overlooked or co-opted. I may choose to sit in a way that occupies the whole chair or spread my belongings on the table in front of me, for example, or stand in a way to take up extra space. Taking up more physical space establishes a sense of parity. In a coaching scenario where I am already in a position of authority, however, I may decide to make a different choice.

Noticing non-verbal communication and taking information from the surrounding environment is naturally prioritized for some. Called "high context" in the culture literature, these individuals constantly register significant meaning in all that is *not* said. A "low-context" person, on the other hand, would make meaning by paying the most attention to words and less to non-verbal cues. Imagine, for example, that you are receiving feedback from your manager. Do you ...?

A. Primarily listen for the key words to understand the message being sent.
B. Primarily pay attention to *how* your manager provides the feedback, including where and when.

A high-context person would answer (B). Note that much of the world operates in a high-context way. The meaning made of the particulars of a given context, however, will vary based on the person and culture.

I've observed hundreds of new coaches in what we call "real play" situations where we ask them to bring real-life cases to practice this model. As they begin the coaching conversation at Step #1, we look for a welcoming tone and the degree to which the coach is truly "taking in" through the senses the coachee sitting directly in front of them. (This is where attention to non-verbal communication and being present overlap.) As the coach relays the coaching topic, the coachee may cross his arms or legs. We ask the coach, did you notice that? While it might be the coachee getting comfortable in his chair, it may also reflect a feeling of discomfort or vulnerability (or something else entirely). But noticing the movement is information and when connected with other data, produces a theory that could be inquired about. Listening with all of the senses requires being fully present, noticing the other person, and acting on that information to determine the next step.

When verbal and non-verbal messages conflict, consider bringing this into the light of day: "I'm sensing that you may not be convinced of this idea," or "How do you feel about what I'm saying?" or "Are you distracted by something I'm saying?" or "I hear you saying yes, but the rest of you seems to say no." In the same way, the coach communicating a consistent message in content and tone eliminates dissonance or distraction that slows trust-building. Coaches, themselves, also need to avoid crossing arms and legs that indicate a psychologically "closed" stance. Keeping your body relaxed will help you deliver a message that is consistent with words about being open to listening.

Finally, the rate of speech is a particularly potent aspect of communication that carries significant information. In regard to rate of speech, most speakers can benefit from slowing down for many reasons:

- Emphasize the topic's import.
- Signal you have time for the other – a sign of respect.
- Make better decisions on what to say next with the extra thinking time you've given yourself.
- Allow for more intentional word choice and tone of voice.

Be Aware of Power Dynamics

We can't avoid the fact that humans – and especially humans in organizations – are obsessed with hierarchy and power. I remember overhearing the beginning of a video coaching session between "Jack," a client, and my partner, David. That particular day David had dressed more casually than usual. When turning on the camera, the first thing the client said, laughing, was, "Hey, you're just a guy in a T-shirt!" Through his casual appearance, the coach was a more accessible, "regular guy," changing the power equilibrium for the coachee.

The coach wants to avoid activating the fight-or-flight part of the brain (the amygdala), which may decide to regain a sense of control which reverberates as "you-versus-me" thinking. If feelings of dependency and vulnerability are evoked, the coachee may pick his favorite form of resistance – deflecting, avoiding, shutting down, denying, or blaming. Any of these reactions slows trust-building and gets in the way of a productive conversation.

On the flip side, sometimes the context calls for a different sort of leveling of the playing field. The aforementioned case about the T-shirt involved two white men. But in dominantly white, male organizations, minority populations may need to reinforce the power dynamic to be effective. A petite, female management consultant I know quite powerfully and effectively takes the CEO's favorite chair every time they meet.

An important strategy for neutralizing power asymmetries (and, importantly, signaling accountability of the coachee for his own learning) is through a technique called "permissioning." Permissioning is the act of pausing to ask for an "OK" before taking the liberty to enter new territory. By presenting a choice, the ownership of decision-making is distributed. For example, "Do you mind if I share an observation with you related to your development?" Note that the person might still feel obliged to agree on account of role power dynamics, but if your tone of voice and pace correspond with your intention to support, providing a choice is more likely to have the desired impact. The way the coach invokes role power will affect the amount of psychological tension and thus the outcome of the conversation. In certain cases, increasing the power distance by making statements without asking permission, for example, can be useful.

Use the Developmental Coaching Model

Those who are already process-minded will especially appreciate how a consistent approach, such as the use of a coaching model, contributes to trust. From a coachee perspective, the repeated experience over time of being listened to and engaged in meaningful topics changes how she relates to the coach, her role, and herself. The coachee learns that the one-on-one coaching conversation is an opportunity to connect, think expansively, and learn, all the while feeling supported and valued.

From a coach perspective, knowing how to guide the conversation instills confidence in himself. When the conversation diverges too far, the coach has a point of reference and knows where to return. A colleague of mine describes the benefit of process models as "flexibility within a framework"; frameworks are meant to support, but never control or constrict those using it.[9] With every use of the model, the manager-coach becomes more competent and develops more confidence in his abilities.

Trust Challenges

After thousands of hours of my own coaching, and having observed hundreds of hours of coaching, I've seen certain trust challenges emerge time and again. Identifying these challenges and providing strategies can help to better prepare the coach, even though every learner will need to fall into similar traps in order to really learn – this is the nature of adult development!

Trust Challenge #1: Not Wanting to Upset a Harmonious Relationship

An ironic aspect about having a harmonious relationship with another person – arguably based on a sense of interpersonal trust – is that we don't count on it. We fear losing the relationship *despite* the existing trust. It's understandable, however. Managing conflict is difficult for so many, and we don't always trust ourselves to manage the moment of disagreement. I have one coaching client who moves mountains to avoid conflict with anyone. He looked me in the eye the other day and said, "I don't make mistakes." I admire his commitment to not having conflict with others, but the pressure must be intense. In coaching scenarios, hesitancy to introduce a topic or provide direct feedback is common, and often manifests as a coach who dances around the topic, not daring to be clear with the coachee about concerns or feelings.

Considerations and Approaches for Trust Challenge #1

Consider that recognizing trust or harmony means a solid (enough) foundation has been poured, and now it's time to stand on it. The payoff for taking the risk is the fact that when two people successfully navigate a challenging topic the relationship gets stronger. Tips on navigating the anxiety of potential conflict:

- Get straight to the coaching topic – within 60-90 seconds in most cases. When coachees have too much time to imagine the purpose of a conversation, they can experience an erosion of trust.
- Separate thoughts from feelings when speaking. For example, "I've prepared feedback for you about your work on the project. Today I want to give that to you so you can know what I noticed, and then to discuss

it together." (Pause for a response but do not start the conversation yet.) Continuing, "At the same time, I'm aware I've never given you much feedback before and I feel concerned you won't be open to it." Then stay present and attentive to hear the reaction and respond with sufficient joining. This opens a larger conversation, which is the point.

■ Address topics as soon as you see them, or notice a pattern of two examples. And do so before your emotions escalate. Bringing up topics as soon as you find yourself pondering them (and definitely before beginning a search for solutions) limits the likelihood for bad feelings, resentments, or the like to become entangled. Don't give concerns the time and environment to develop inside of you. Waiting complicates everything.

Trust Challenge #2: The Coachee Is Highly Resistant

As mentioned, resistance is often thought of as something negative or bad, but is entirely natural and healthy – it keeps us out of harm's way. I resist mushrooms, being told what to do, and having too much routine in my day. Why? Because my experiences inform me that these situations are not good for me (no matter if it's true or not). To change means letting go of what was done before, provoking relatively unpleasant feelings of tension and uncertainty due to an admission of lack of knowledge, pride, or other internal phenomenon.[10] Instead of pushing, fighting, or avoiding, think of resistance as an opportunity to learn about the perspective – hear the person, demonstrate understanding of the concerns, and harness the resistant energy to build trust.

Considerations and Approaches for Trust Challenge #2

■ Ask yourself what you can do to demonstrate and reinforce the two rules of trust presented earlier: Have the best interest of the coachee at heart, and use your competence on the topic of resistance to get curious and learn.

■ Take responsibility for your part in the situation as you introduce the topic (Step #2), such as: "I think our communication has not been very effective for some time, in part because I've not listened to you closely enough and I've underestimated the complexity of your project. I think you've needed more guidance from me and more air cover. Do you feel that way?" In the Contracting phase, the coach takes the time to articulate, discuss, negotiate meaning, make agreements, and so on, while being curious about differences in perspective.

■ Consider whether the source of the coachee's resistance corresponds to willingness or ability. If the coachee is *unwilling* (attitude), focus on understanding why and illuminate the personal benefits. If you deem the coachee is *unable* to change (skills), put the focus on identifying the specific skills needed and corresponding learning strategies.

Trust Challenge #3: You Know "The Answer"

It's common for subject matter experts – whether functional, industry, or other – to consider their professional expertise as the basis for competency in coaching. While having some contextual grounding for a particular topic can be helpful, being an expert on the topic being discussed can also interfere with the coaching process. When we know too much, we speak from our own paradigms and already-lived solutions. Imagine, for example, a coachee struggling with attention to detail – something you are good at or have worked hard to learn. The coach will likely be tempted to solve or give advice. This kind of "help" often disempowers, taking away the learning opportunity of the other. Of course, it's seductive for the coach to solve, and the coachee will often *want* you to solve it, but neither leads to development.

Considerations and Approaches for Trust Challenge #3

■ Remain curious about the coachee's experience. Separate your own sense of what works with what the coachee thinks will work.

■ Outsource the thinking. When you see a coaching topic, don't think about it for too long. Share your unfinished thought. Bring up topics and help connect the dots, but not the solutions. When coaches wait too long to address something, brains go into overdrive and undermine coachees' ability to learn and come up with their own solutions.

Trust Challenge #4: Remote Coaching

When the relationship with a coachee develops remotely (via video conference and over the phone), both coach and coachee can expect ongoing surprises and disappointments. Hundreds of assumptions are made – often incorrect – which conspire to keep the relationship off balance. Collaboration feels difficult and inefficient. What's missing is sufficient experiences in common, and thus knowledge gaps are everywhere: no in-person encounters in hallways or meeting rooms; limited overlapping work hours defying easy connections; time zones affecting energy levels; communication preferences not accounted for; incompatible or unreliable technologies interrupting perfectly laid plans, to name a few. It's like painting a landscape with only reds and greens: What's the rest of the picture?

Considerations and Approaches for Trust Challenge #4

- Use video conferencing to increase the amount of information exchanged during each conversation. Information from the visual field helps build curiosity, attentiveness, and more connection.
- Agree on communication preferences for different situations (plus expectations on frequency).
- Make time for check-in calls to discuss the coachee's *experience* of his work and his current projects: What's working? What's not? What is enjoyable? Why? Not enjoyable? Why? When the conversation moves to aspects of the work tasks or projects themselves, bring it back to the coachee's feelings about the work.
- Weave in high-leverage questions that can be used to build your knowledge about the person, one conversation at a time. See the next chapter for a list called "What Makes you Tick?"
- Realize the importance of *task-based trust* when working remotely. Research shows that task completion, responsiveness, and follow-through have more weight in building trust than for co-located colleagues.
- Become attuned to knowing when to switch back and forth between task and process. Is it time to build a plan, or is it time to share feelings about the collaboration or the project? Research shows that successful remote leaders are particularly adept at this, which extends to coaches as well.

Trust Challenge #5: You Are Completely Stuck! Who Shifts?

Sometimes relationships feel completely frozen. Perhaps you feel you've tried everything. In relationship stalemates, the natural question is "Who shifts?" No matter – it's always a dynamic between individuals and the larger context that conspire to create the present reality.

Considerations and Approaches for Trust Challenge #5

- Make the frozen relationship the topic of the coaching conversation. Ask yourself what the other person wants or needs from you and bring a theory with you about why (as described in the next chapter). Think about everything from the other's point of view. Consider writing out, and practice, your first sentences to ensure your words are as precise as possible. Consider role playing with someone who knows the person, or recording yourself and playing it back to check your pace and tone of voice.

- Find neutral, third-party help from someone who is trusted by both you and the coachee. I once played the facilitator with two members of the same leadership team – the director of plant operations and a younger, rising star. The director had played a mentoring role, and the two were very close friends. However, the relationship was compromised by a perceived breach of trust and they hadn't recovered. Through individual coaching conversations I had with each, it became clear both were interested to resolve the conflict but neither would take the first step. So, with their approval, we held a three-way meeting where they worked together to draw the timeline of their relationship and tell me their story. Within a few hours, the relationship was on track and I watched them return to harmony and friendship in the weeks that followed. The third-party role was to set the boundaries and guidelines, intervene as necessary, and to serve as a witness for each of them as they worked.

The Time It Takes

We've covered in this chapter just a sliver of all there is to say about trust. Perhaps the biggest obstacle is that of time. We ask ourselves, how can we add more hours to our already-full day? As such, I end with a story. For 3 years, I worked as a board member at a local nonprofit. The organization had taken up a significant amount of my time, but was fulfilling in that I was achieving the goals I had established for myself when deciding to join. At some point, my priorities shifted and I decided to resign. Surprisingly, the hours were reabsorbed so quickly back into my life that I never felt a blip of free time after my departure; The time was consumed by the rest of what I was managing. "How did I *ever* accomplish all my board work?" I asked myself.

I was reminded, then, that there is always time for what we deeply want to do. From a manager-coach perspective, finding time to build relationship and trust is simply a choice. If you want to experiment, you *will* find the time.

Notes

1 Sullian, P. (2016, June 10). Deciding if a financial advisor is right for the job. *The New York Times*. https://www.nytimes.com/2016/06/11/your-money/deciding-if-a-financial-adviser-is-right-for-the-job.html.
2 Covey, S. R., & Merrill, R. R. (2006). *The Speed of Trust: The One Thing That Changes Everything*. New York, NY: Simon and Schuster.
3 Ibid.
4 Bridges, W. (2009). *Managing Transitions: Making the Most of Change*. Cambridge, MA: Da Capo Press.
5 This is another wonderful concept – "Getting the fundamentals right gives you a much greater chance of getting lucky" – from my tennis coach extraordinaire, Issa Cohen. It's simply amazing how many of his tennis wisdoms correlate closely with the principles of developmental coaching.
6 Berlyne, D. E. (1954). A theory of human curiosity. *British Journal of Psychology, 45*(3), 180-191.
7 Intensity of motivation is highest when a person believes they can close a knowledge gap (and reduction of feelings of tension). For more information: Loewenstein, G. (1994). The psychology of curiosity: A review and reinterpretation. *Psychological Bulletin, 116*(1), 75.
8 Mehrabian, A. (1981). *Silent Messages: Implicit Communication of Emotions and Attitudes*. Belmont, CA: Wadsworth.
9 My colleague and friend is Paul LeBoffe, LeBoffe & Associates.
10 Litman, J. A., & Jimerson, T. L. (2004). The measurement of curiosity as a feeling of deprivation. *Journal of Personality Assessment, 82*(2), 147-157.

Chapter 4

Phase II: Contracting

Some people will never learn anything...because they understand everything too soon.

— Alexander Pope

When the coach guides the client to identify and agree upon a developmental goal which is of high interest to the client, this is called Contracting. This phase – Steps #2, #3, and #4 together – will answer key questions that establish what the coaching will be about:

- What's the need/want?
- How is that connected to the client's development?
- What's the benefit of doing so?
- Do we agree on the developmental goal?
- How can the coach be most useful in this conversation?

As these questions are discussed and resolved, a psychological agreement – or contract – is being established between the coach and client. It's the conversation *before* the conversation. Like written contracts, both parties provide input since neither person has the whole story: The *coach* has her own observations, self-awareness, feelings, and experiences, as well as knowledge of the coaching process, while the *client* brings self-awareness, feelings, experiences, and motivations. By the end of this phase, the client has identified and taken responsibility for a developmental goal. Interest in the topic should be high, unleashing enough psychological energy and focus to move to the next phase of the coaching, when considering *how* to move toward the goal.

Managers new to coaching may initially perceive the contracting phase as much more process-oriented or formal because a relatively large amount of time is spent determining what will be discussed and how *before* diving in to address it, when so many managers are used to taking this communication shortcut. This is understandable: Fast-paced work environments are exceedingly pragmatic, and the communication default is to move quickly to solutions. *But the contracting phase is what distinguishes coaching from other kinds of workplace communication; it's the essence of coaching because of the time taken to examine the coachee's underlying beliefs, values, and assumptions, and tying the business issue to the coachee's development.* For this to happen, the coach will need to steer the client away from simple problem-solving, sometimes referred to as "single-loop learning." The term, originating from Chris Argyris, business theorist and Professor Emeritus at Harvard Business School, described single-loop learning as appropriate for situations requiring simple fixes, while "double-loop learning" is focused on more complex scenarios which evolve and change as one begins to take action and which benefit from looking at what's underneath the presenting issue.[1] In Contracting, the way in which the challenge is defined will contribute to the outcome. The work of Phase II is to explicitly connect the presenting business issue to the motivation and desired development of the coachee.

The following explanation on Contracting is organized into two sections, beginning with scenarios when the *coach* initiates the topic. We call this "coach-led coaching." These are situations when the coach has seen an opportunity for the coachee to develop in some way. Then, we'll turn to scenarios when the *client* initiates the topic, which we call "client-led coaching." Depending on who brings up the topic, Contracting, and Step #2 in particular, will unfold slightly differently, each with unique considerations for the coach. Let's look at each.

Coach-Led Contracting (Steps #2, #3, and #4)

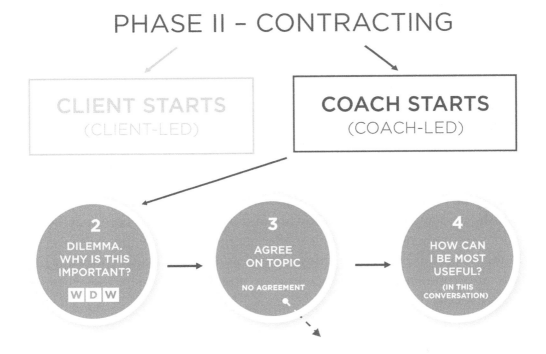

PHASE II – CONTRACTING

CLIENT STARTS
(CLIENT-LED)

COACH STARTS
(COACH-LED)

2
DILEMMA.
WHY IS THIS
IMPORTANT?
W D W

3
AGREE
ON TOPIC
NO AGREEMENT

4
HOW CAN
I BE MOST
USEFUL?
(IN THIS
CONVERSATION)

Coach-Led Contracting Is Like Setting the Table

Beginning with an analogy, consider that Phases I and II of coaching is like the experience of having an esteemed acquaintance to your home for lunch. When the person arrives for the first time, you are likely to do two things: Help the person feel comfortable, and talk about the meal. As you imagine the scenario that follows, avoid evaluating whether this is exactly how you would host someone, and instead consider it an example of how a coaching conversation could feel and sound.

Here's the scene. You've invited an esteemed acquaintance – someone you want to get to know better – to your home on a weekend afternoon. Because you ostensibly care enough about that person to invite them, you've thought about the experience ahead of time. You've considered your calendar and made the invitation. Ahead of their arrival, you've pondered the dishes you'll serve, shopped for ingredients, and prepared them. The day of arrival, you've checked that the physical space is comfortable. When your guest arrives, you welcome him and tell him you're happy he's there. As he comes into the room, you notice his body language and disposition. You suggest he sit in the comfortable chair, wanting him to feel relaxed. This is Step #1 "Establish a Climate of Trust," because you're demonstrating that you care about the person and have his best interests at heart. Your actions also signal that you've prepared a nutritious and (hopefully) satisfying meal to be enjoyed in the immediate future.

Step #2: Dilemma. Why Is This Important?

Continuing from our analogy above, now imagine the meal is on the table. You've prepared three dishes – one main dish and two side dishes. The main dish is the developmental dilemma and is the main reason for the conversation. The other side dishes are for "making sense" of the meal and are important for the main dish to taste good. As you sit together, you describe each dish to your guest – what they are and a few details. There may be questions (ingredients? how was it made? allergies?). Ideally, there is curiosity and interest on the part of the guest. You're a good cook and you want him to taste and comment! (Figure 4.1). In coaching, we abbreviate these three dishes as **WDW**:

- The **W**ant or need (about the business or a behavior)
- The developmental **D**ilemma (a *personal, different* want or need that gets in the way)
- The **W**IFM (how the coachee would answer to "What's in It for Me?")

Figure 4.1   The main dish is always the "developmental Dilemma." The two side dishes – the "Want" and "WIFM" – make a complete meal and make the main dish "taste good."

The coach can present any of the dishes first, but we recommend using them in order until you feel ready to experiment. The goal of Step #2, then, is to talk to the coachee about each dish because you've prepared them each to be served together. Let's look at each dish.

W: Identify the "Want"

In coach-led coaching, the manager-coach tells the client what she wants, which is a specific opportunity related to the business or the coachee's effectiveness, followed by why it's important. The coach begins, therefore, by introducing the first side dish.

The want can be derived from the business ("I want Joe to streamline this process") or be developmental in nature ("I want Joe to delegate more"). Both statements are 100% valid as a starting place. However, if a "business want" comes to mind, the manager-coach must take it one step further to *personalize* it. What does a streamlined process have to do *with Joe*? The coach might specify "I want Joe to pay more attention to how people and resources are utilized." (The want could include psychological or emotional renditions also, such as "I want Joe to find ways to let go of work he has already mastered to take on new challenges.") Articulating the want generally requires some consideration from the coach because she knows the goal of Step #2 is not only to solve a business problem. The coach may choose to frame the want in developmental terms from the beginning, and use the business situation as context.

Once identifying the "personalized want," the coach articulates *why* this is desired. The "why" is especially important as a place to address the broader business context, which could change our acronym to W*w*DW: want, *why*, dilemma, WIFM, but for simplicity, we keep the model WDW.

Coach-Led Case #1: Julian Has an Unsatisfied Customer

The following case about Julian will be used throughout the rest of the book. Here the context of the case is introduced and begins a sample statement corresponding to Step #2.

Imagine your direct report, Julian, is a strategic account manager in sales. He's been unable to appease Customer Jane, who is unsatisfied with the product delivered last week. Julian hasn't discussed it with you, and you believe Julian is distracted with other tasks and is not reacting quickly enough to Customer Jane, which concerns you. Your instinct is to solve this problem as quickly as possible, but you slow yourself down to consider the desired outcome: What do you ultimately want? The "business want" that comes to mind is "a happy customer!" But remembering you are a manager-coach and this is Julian's opportunity to learn, you ask yourself, broadly speaking, what you want for *him*, which will also meet the business outcome you want. Using your observations of Julian, thinking back over the last year of customer interactions, you feel he could pay more attention to managing the customer's overall experience because you've noticed his communication is reactive, reaching out primarily when he has good news or in response to a specific request. That Julian build stronger relationships with his external clients in a more proactive way is your "personal want" for Julian. You write this down as part of your preparation, and then, you add why this is important in the current context (for the business, for the customer, for the team, etc). You know to avoid the abstract and high-level "why," such as "our customers pay our bills." You then address Julian:

> I'm concerned about the situation with Jane and her dissatisfaction. It's not the first time she's been disappointed in us, as a company. I'd like to hear how we can ensure her satisfaction with our product. But this conversation is firstly about you, so before talking about Jane, I'd like to use this as a case study for learning. (…) Julian, you do a terrific job of aligning the internal resources to meet customer needs, helping us with solid, on-time delivery; that's a credit to your efforts. We've discussed this strength of yours in the past. Applying those same skills externally would likely reverse the kinds of situations we have with Jane, who may lament her experience with us this week. As you know, one of our strategic directions is providing extraordinary customer service and I'd like to explore this with you. Julian, I'd like you to provide each customer a consistent experience that exceeds their expectations all year long."

In the above opening, the coach has expressed a "want" and a "why." She stops here to get a reaction while keeping in mind her goal is to get to the main dish, the specific developmental "dilemma."

Challenges with the "Want"

■ *The coach is tempted to use negative language,* or *what she doesn't want.* The language of deficiencies is deeply engrained into the lexicon of business; it's difficult to avoid it entirely. But with a bit of reflection, the coach can often convert her language into an aspect of a desired future state – *moving toward* something. The subtle change of *moving toward something positive* is more generative than pondering how to *get away from* something, in this case, reactive or sporadic communication. While at times we may need to hear the negative to draw attention to what will impede us, these complaints communicate a desire to "fix someone," like a problem to be solved instead of the human realm of learning, growing, thriving, and flourishing. In doing so, the topic changes from a language of *deficiencies* to the language of *opportunity.*

■ *The "want" sometimes does not engage because the topic is too big or too small.* Making the "want" a manageable size is called "scoping." Scoping is the set of boundaries that define the extent of the topic. For example, "I want you to get to work on time" is too small and, as such, surely won't engage the client. The conversation will result in problem-solving. On the other extreme, "I want to discuss your personality" is too general (and inappropriate). The want is scoped too large when there are dozens of directions the conversation could go. Instead, a right-sized want might be, "I want you to be a role model with regards to observing agreements." Note that changing the language does not concern finding fancier ways to discuss "getting to work on time." Instead, it's about broadening the topic to challenge the coachee at a different level that would truly move the needle on the coachee's effectiveness as a leader. In the case of Julian, a topic which is too small is, "I want you to have weekly check-ins with clients." This is a directive and micro-management. "I want you to change the way you work so we avoid dissatisfied customers" may be too vague. Poorly scoped wants will make it more difficult to coach. Other potential "personal wants" for Julian could be:
  – To build closer relationships with clients
  – To stay calm with clients who are negative or frustrated
  – To advocate more effectively on behalf of the customer
  – To become highly skilled in managing conflict
  – To gain more technical aptitude in ways that build trust with clients

■ *The coach introduces the want too slowly, eroding trust.* On one of my first consulting projects, I had something difficult to say to a client. I spent a number of minutes in a kind of warm-up – waiting to feel a flow between me and my client and searching for how to broach the topic. As I stalled, I could see the level of trust going down. When

I finally was ready to give my message, my client was seriously perturbed. The act of moving slowly through the beginning of the conversation went from a pleasant exchange, to suspicion, to irritation. I realized I was not fully prepared in what I would say and was unsure of my message. The learning was etched in my mind for the rest of time: Tell your coachee the purpose of the meeting and topic right away – within 90 seconds in most cases – to avoid the unintentional erosion of trust. Simply remind yourself to prepare, have a caring attitude, and relay the message.

D: Dilemma – Your Theory

After establishing the "personal want" (and why it's important), the coach turns to the main dish – the developmental dilemma. In coach-led coaching, the coach introduces a theory about the coachee. What attitude, behavior, ability, or limitation is getting in the way of the want? Stated again as something positive to move toward, what other need is working at cross-purposes? These two elements constitute the "developmental dilemma." If, per our example, the coach wants Julian to have a consistent, systematic approach to communicating with customers (in order to provide a better experience), the theoretical dilemma might be that Julian has a propensity to focus on internal customers because, as an introvert, those internal relationships take priority. This developmental dilemma is based on thoughtful consideration by the coach and is meant to drive the conversation deeper. The coach may be incorrect in her theory, but the statement has done its job to signal the start of a developmental conversation. An incorrect theory will likely prompt the coachee to describe his *real* dilemma, or at least start the thinking process.

"THE STORY I MAKE UP ... "

It's important to remember that a theory is only a theory. Manager-coaches are not diagnosing or deciding for the coachee what's getting in their way. Using the expression "the story I make up" suggests the coach is forwarding an educated guess instead of a fact. As such, it potentially lowers resistance that may arise. Ideally, the coachee feels more free to update the incorrect assumption and provide the "real" story. This is another signal that the coachee defines his own development.

If Julian's manager doesn't have a theory – she can't think of what other force is at play – the coach simply asks: "Julian, what gets in your way of providing the same treatment to our external customers that you so adeptly provide to your internal customers?" Perhaps Julian then reveals, for example, that she prefers less communication to keep any potential conflict to a minimum. The coach should continue to ask "Why?" and then "Why is *that*?" to get at his underlying assumptions and the real developmental dilemma.[2] (With practice, the coach learns to reframe any statement to the positive, "You want to maintain calm or harmonious relationships whenever you can," which leads to a deeper discussion, all while keeping away from the language of deficiencies.)

When asking why a few times, it's easy for the coach to find herself in the territory of the emotions. Asking why someone is afraid to hear bad news, for example, will require a conversation about how it feels upon hearing bad news. The ability to speak about feelings will depend on her level of self-development and leadership "range" – the ability to show up in a spectrum of ways to correspond to different situations. The leader's range has a direct impact on how flexible her methods can be in developing others. As such, the development of the coach is paramount to the development of the coachee.

THE WORDS YOU CHOOSE

Throughout this book, you see examples and dialogues in the author's voice based on one person's context and experiences. You may say to yourself, "I would say it differently." Readers should know that they can find their own way, with their own style and voice. At the same time, some of what's recommended will feel uncomfortable because new coaches are adding new concepts – and corresponding language – to one's repertoire. While some may sound odd to one's own ears at first, this is the nature of learning.

Contrasting Dilemmas and Problems

Why use the terminology of "dilemmas" instead of "problems" and their underlying obstacles? The answer to this question is essential for managers who want to promote transformational learning at work. A dilemma involves two or more options that seem to be incompatible – one belief that seemingly gets in the way of another: *Do I continue to focus on my personal development this year or do I focus on my family obligations?* Notice how they are framed as alternatives. Framed as a dilemma, these aspects are placed in relation to one another, complementary and, quite possibly, both achievable: "How do I focus on my personal development this year while keeping a focus on my family obligations?" Dilemmas are meant to be managed, not solved, which is why coaching requires a different mindset than that of problem-solving. We're not seeking a simple decision or behavior change, because there are important and complex dynamics to consider. To manage a dilemma requires a change of a paradigm or a redefinition of a value system.

A *societal* example of a dilemma is that of the smog level in your city which is too high on a winter's day. Addressed as a *problem*, the local government could restrict traffic in the city which would immediately lower the number of particulates in the air that day or week. Solving a problem is often expedient and effective short term. But this solution will create other problems, such as overcrowded public transportation systems, or preventing people from working or shopping. A *dilemma*, on the other hand, requires zooming out to see more forces at play: We all want clean air. And we all also want to have our own cars. (Notice that dilemmas are both written as two desirable options.) To address this challenge in a sustainable way, we would need to consider our value systems. There is no "correct" response; a dilemma cannot be 100% resolved, but choices can be made to manage the dilemma.

Let's look at another situation in line with coaching. Imagine I decide I want to spend time acting more strategically, but have a long-standing pattern of spending significant time ticking items off my to-do list. Solving this issue like a *problem* might be going to the office 45 minutes earlier several days a week, to allow myself time to reflect and think strategically. This *could* work, but more likely this approach will not address the fact that because I'm so oriented to taking action, I will easily succumb to using those extra minutes to get things done that I didn't complete the day before. While it might help to arrive to work earlier, doing so doesn't necessarily address my underlying orientation of keeping myself busy with tasks. When the coach can think in terms of dilemmas – most of which involve the coachee's emotional and psychological inner-life – conversations better expose the root cause and prevailing assumptions, which allow for a thoughtful reexamination.

DILEMMAS ARE TWO ENDS OF A
CONTINUUM, AND BOTH DESIRABLE

A coaching client of mine talked about feeling low energy and disengagement. She felt in a rut of simply fulfilling tasks for others all day. When I asked her what she wanted, she said to feel energized by spending time being a strategic thought leader, and having her voice heard in the organization. I suggested the dilemma as wanting a different balance between the amount of time spent following versus leading, and her eyes lit up in recognition. We explored each side thoroughly to identify and scope the topic further. The shift she was seeking might be charted on a continuum (below) as moving from A to B.

Follow Others ……..A…………………………B…………… Lead Others

Challenges with the Developmental Dilemma

- *The coach is only comfortable in speaking from the cognitive, rational part of the brain.* Supporting people through the psychological and emotional experience of working in demanding organizations is part of leading in any organization today. In fact, given the amount of change most employees are experiencing, it's surprising that the rate of overwhelm, exhaustion, and burnout at work isn't actually higher. When managers can share their feelings, demonstrate empathy, or discuss their intentions, they demonstrate the ability to engage on the range of human emotions and normalize the expression of feelings at work. Importantly, expression of one's feelings releases internal tension and speeds up how people adapt to their environment.[3] Said differently (and this is counterintuitive), change is accelerated when individuals express their feelings – even negative ones – because doing so supports movement toward accepting the new reality.
- *The coach doesn't have a theory about what other need is at play.* In these cases, the manager can spend more time noticing the coachee's patterns, especially what they do in moments of difficulty or stress. Alternatively, the manager-coach can just ask the coachee.
- *The client doesn't agree with the theory or its level of importance that the coach has put forward.* Respond with curiosity. There is no need to abandon your want unless the client provides new information that nullifies your own. Ask what they think is most important from their point

of view. If expecting resistance, have data ready to legitimize your state-ments and perceptions to avoid negotiation about what is true or not.

■ *There is no dilemma.* Sometimes bringing up a topic and a theory about a developmental dilemma is met with surprise or acceptance. For exam-ple, the coach explains that she wants the coachee to bring more legiti-macy to the change initiatives he is driving. The dilemma that the coach sees is a reticence to spend time on data analysis. If the coachee agrees and sees no constraint in doing so, then the exchange was simply feed-back that promoted self-awareness.

W: WIFM (What's in It for Me?)

The second side dish is the answer to "What's in It for Me?" or WIFM. The coach presents the benefit of the development *from the perspective of the coachee.* A thoughtful reflection of the question based on what the coach knows about the coachee goes a long way to take the conversation deeper and build trust. Since people are perfectly able to change when perceiving a clear, personal benefit, the goal to this side dish is to explicitly and con-cretely discuss the coachee's intrinsic motivational factor(s) to address the developmental dilemma. Making statements about the benefits of the devel-opmental goal must be specific to the person and go well beyond generali-ties of "being more effective" or "help you advance in the organization."

A case study about motivation involves a friend's sister, Elaine, who was apprenticing at a hair salon. At an early stage in her training, one of her tasks was to fold towels. At her performance review, her manager asked her to look more cheerful as she worked, saying customers preferred smiles. Elaine understood the point, but the request left her cold. Of course, while any manager wants happy-looking employees, the manager needed to think harder about the want, what smiling has to do with her development, and what Elaine might get out of doing so. Moreover, the lack of smiles hope-fully prompts curiosity about whether Elaine is happy in her role and how she is doing overall.

A common difficulty to moving through Step #2 is the lack of a WIFM – the manager doesn't know enough about what intrinsically motivates others and, therefore, doesn't really know why the coachee would be interested to change. (The default of "so she can keep her job!" tends to be uttered in exasperation, but this isn't what we have in mind.) If coaches want to engage others, they need to know their coachee's internal drivers.

WIFMs generally connect to the coachee's broad goals, such as career development, learning, positive impact on the business or customer, a collegial environment, and even the relationship with the coach.

In one prominent study, researchers found seven critical employee motivators that drive "attraction" (hiring) or "retention" (staying) across all major segments and labor markets globally. For our purposes, we focus on the circle on the right, those elements that motivate employees to remain engaged in their role.[4]

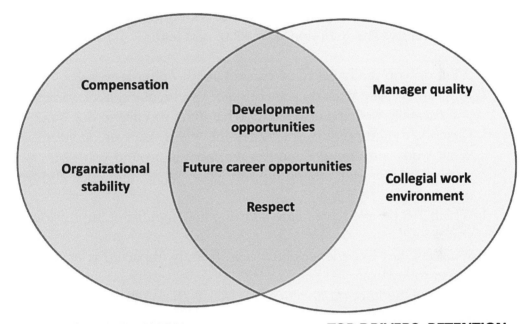

TOP DRIVERS: ATTRACTION   **TOP DRIVERS: RETENTION**

Engaging employees: what matters?
Across 38 employee value proposition attributes, 7 are critical for driving attraction (recruiting and hiring) or commitment (retention) across all major segments and labor markets. Respondents are from all industries, functions, continents.

The above diagram helps to orient a coach regarding what motivates employees. However, while any of these aforementioned WIFMs are true for *someone*, the specific WIFM must be meaningful for that individual at that time. Taking a random guess will not lead to the deeper conversation that engages the coachee. These motivational categories can, however, provoke more questions. How, for example, is "respect" defined and demonstrated from the coachee's point of view? What constitutes "manager quality" in the coachee's eyes? What kind of development is appealing? What are the coachee's long-term goals? In other words, for coaches to powerfully frame the WIFM, coaches need to know what their coachees care about most.

WHAT MAKES YOU TICK?

The following questions can help you learn what motivates others. Choose a few favorites and create moments to engage on these topics. Don't treat this as a checklist, however. Allow plenty of time to really explore and to get to know the other person. Go back with another question at your next opportunity. The intention is to relax and learn.

1. What do you really get most excited about doing at work?
2. In your job today, what do you consider your unique skillset, something you do really well and also enjoy? What don't you like to do? Why?
3. Describe a high point in your work life when you were at your best. What were you doing? What was happening around you? Who was involved? How did others support you? What difference did you make?
4. Which 1–2 people have made a lasting and significant impression on you? Why?
5. What few key experiences have significantly impacted your work or career today?
6. What are the important values and beliefs that guide you in your life today? Can you provide a few examples?
7. What are a few vitally important things that I should know about you?
8. How do you build trust with others?
9. What are your career aspirations? Why are these important to you?
10. When you're anxious or stressed, what does it look like to others around you? How can others be of support to you during those times?
11. What's one thing I could do to help you be more successful? Why is that important to you?

Challenges with the WIFM

■ *Manager-coaches don't know the coachee's WIFM.* In the moment of coaching, coaches may need to spend adequate time exploring "What would be the benefit to you to [learn this]?" Ideally the coach has good insight on the question ahead of time. If not, the coach opens the question without the need to convince or influence.

■ *The coach uses a salary increase or job promotion as a WIFM.* While most everyone wants more money and influence, the problem with using these motivators is a lack of downstream thinking. Managers may be inadvertently communicating a *quid pro quo*, barter, or promise. When the time comes, the coach may determine that a different person is a better fit for the role. Or business conditions change, leaving the coach's hands tied and resulting in a coachee feeling betrayed. It's dangerous territory. Keep career conversations regarding rewards like promotions separate from developmental conversations. Mixing the two often ends badly. Each conversation has a different purpose and timing. As for salary increases as motivation, financial incentives typically neither make for happier nor more productive employees.[5] The caveat to this scenario is when the client feels their pay or job level is below market rate, which becomes an issue of fairness.

■ *The coach feels that using motivational factors is manipulative.* Occasionally, manager-coaches feel suspicious about using WIFMs in the context of coaching, saying it feels disingenuous or manipulative. This is not the case as long as the primary goal of the conversation is to support the coachee's needs, development, and growth, and the coach is transparent about how any change impacts the coach and organization. Manipulation occurs when coaches hold back relevant information, such as how the coach, herself, or the organization benefits. If the mutual benefit is clear to all, there is no conflict of interest. In fact, that coach, coachee, and organization all get their needs met is called alignment and does not indicate a lack of integrity.

How Does a Coach-Led WDW Sound?

Below are two examples of coach-led coaching through WDW, stopping just at Step #3 ("Agreement on the Topic"). In the first example, you'll see only the "voice" of the coach to keep your focus on the coach's use of WDW.

Example of Steps #1–2 – Alicia Focuses on External Customers

(*Coach Eric to Alicia*) I'd like to talk to you today about a developmental opportunity I see for you to take your skills to the next level, which pertains to your passion for customer satisfaction. Are you ok to have a conversation now on this topic?

(...)

First, I want to acknowledge and appreciate your leadership in the team in this regard, specifically your consistent orientation to the customer in everything we do. Do you see your contribution in the team like I do? (**Step 1: Establish a climate of trust**)

(...)

(Respond to Alicia, and move toward the WDW) I scheduled this meeting because I want to draw your attention to an aspect of customer satisfaction that could make your impact greater, but pertains to your peers. Let me explain: I would like you to collaborate more fluidly with your cross-functional peers (**want**). As an example, I received a message Monday and Wednesday of this week from the product engineer who didn't have adequate information about the customer specifications from you, which caused a lot of extra work for him. The engineer took significant time to get involved when it wasn't his role and seemed reluctant to speak with you about it (**why it's important**). I was reminded of my experience of you in the team meetings; I believe you keep your distance from others. My theory is that you want to spend your time and energy communicating and building relationships with customers, because you are motivated to make large, visible, top-line impact to the company. To you, working closely with peers takes valuable time away from your focus on external customers. Is this how you see it? (**developmental dilemma**)

(... Alicia is hesitant, perhaps wondering how much to share or how much to trust, but feels she is receptive to hear more. The coach can pause to explore thus far, or move to the WIFM because it might help move them forward.)

I also believe you care about the team's perception of you. It ties with your goals of being seen as a highly competent communicator, in general. I believe there are ways to collaborate internally which can simultaneously generate large, visible, top-line impact (**WIFM**).

(...)

(Eric and Alicia discuss until they agree on the developmental dilemma, which may be different than what the coach laid out. The coach moves to Step #3, "Agreement on the Topic")

Example of Step #2 WDW – Following up on a Prior Coaching Conversation

In this example, consider the dialogue with responses from the coachee. In practice, each time a coachee responds, the coach decides how long to discuss each point as they move through the model. For reasons of practicality, exchanges are kept relatively short here. In addition, notice the element of proactive engagement by the coach, who uses open-ended questions to encourage the coachee to engage further.

Coach Ted to Lorena: At our January meeting, you'll recall that we discussed that one career goal of yours was to ensure more work-life balance, avoiding stress where possible, by staying on top of your goals each week so as not to fall behind. How's your progress?

Lorena: I've made some progress but I'm also hitting some obstacles. Overall, it's going better, though.

Ted: Interesting. Can you say more about the progress and also the obstacles?

Lorena: At least twice this month I've missed deadlines, but in general I'm following my time management processes more.

Ted: I've noticed how ready you are with your status reports in meetings this month. Bravo! Is that your experience, too? (...). I also noticed those few instances when you missed deadlines. What are you learning so far? (**establishing more trust, promoting more reflection**)

Lorena: When I take time to write out my goals daily and weekly, I definitely stay more focused. And I still easily get sucked into a lot of tasks that don't correspond to my goals.

Ted: You said you "get sucked in." Is part of the challenge of managing your day also due to the difficulty of saying "no" or, perhaps, being unclear about your priorities?

Lorena: I have a hard time saying "no."

Ted: You sound clear about that. How would you articulate what you are saying you want for yourself?

Lorena: I want to be more aware of how and why I say "yes" when I shouldn't (**want**). I suppose I don't want to disappoint people.

Ted: It sounds like you want to both help others be successful but also help yourself be successful. (**dilemma**) Do you agree with that? (...) I think many people struggle with this. If you were able to do this, how would your life be better? What would change for you? (**WIFM**)

(Lorena begins to explore the benefits, with Ted encouraging more and more angles. He wants her to find out how important this goal is to her success and happiness. If and when Ted sees her motivation well established he moves to Step #3, Agreement on the Topic. He aims to solidify the goal as a topic of ongoing development for her.)

In the scripted comments from Ted, notice the ways the coach keeps the conversation going, using both a *segue word or statement and a follow-up question* (in either order) as he works to establish a dilemma and a clear WIFM. The segue is a kind of "joining," discussed in Chapter 3 on the topic of accelerating trust. Here the coach supports the coachee to continue to share. Note that by eliminating the segue, the question can feel directive, lack empathy, or evoke resistance. To change directions in the conversation, check with the coachee which signals that this conversation is ultimately theirs to steer.

SEGUES TO PROMOTE MORE ENGAGEMENT

Sample questions of how to encourage the coachee to continue sharing and the coach learning[6]:

1. How so? I didn't see that coming.
2. Really? Tell me more … If you're comfortable.
3. Curious, how did that make you feel?
4. That's interesting, and then what?
5. Why is that? If you don't mind me asking.
6. And? I want to hear the rest.
7. That makes sense. What else?
8. I'm learning a lot. Can I go back to something that caught my attention?

Analyzing the Mechanics of Step #2

At this point in your discovery of coaching, you'll notice the introduction of formatted tables to break down the mechanics of coaching. Dialogues may better convey the spirit and tone, but tables provide a clear look at the coaching elements – the bare bones – and how they link together. As you analyze how an initial statement ("presenting topic") could evolve into the components of WDW, keep in mind that you will overlay, of course, your personal finesse and style – trust-building statements, the use of pacing and intonation, and the way you navigate WDW – while also listening and integrating new information as it's revealed. In Table 4.1, consider the four, distinct, presenting topics with an accompanying example of WDW. There are no "correct" conversations; there are innumerable paths to reach any given outcome. Finally, these examples are written to correspond to either a coach-led or a client-led coaching situation.

Table 4.1   Examples of Step #2

	The Want … (What does the coach want the client to move toward…and why?)	*Developmental Dilemma (Value, belief or assumption at play that gets in the way of the want)*	*WIFM (What would intrinsically motivate the client to pursue this developmental dilemma?)*
Presenting Topic	*Step #2 (WDW)*		
1. Diana spends a lot of time on emails and meetings	Be more strategic; Spend time to reflect and act on issues critical to the business long term. Why important? Fire-fighting does not replace long-term solutions	**Manage expectations of the internal stakeholders who send many requests for information**	Be seen as an enterprise-wide thinker; become a more visionary leader
2. Marcos feels resentful and angry at the R&D director for being so difficult to work with	Improve relationship with R&D director. Why important? Collaboration is not optional; Business results are required	**Say "no" to those who push too hard or are inflexible**	Respecting own needs (establishing boundaries) will recalibrate the relationship. Ability to manage conflict will help in all aspects of client's life.

(*Continued*)

Table 4.1 (*Continued*)   Examples of Step #2

Presenting Topic	The Want … (What does the coach want the client to move toward…and why?)	Developmental Dilemma (Value, belief or assumption at play that gets in the way of the want)	WIFM (What would intrinsically motivate the client to pursue this developmental dilemma?)
	Step #2 (WDW)		
3. Janos is overloaded with customer work	Improve work-life balance through better time-management. Why important? Missed deadlines; dissatisfied customers; potential burnout	**Thinking outside the box** is challenging; Feeling of "I don't know how to change my situation"	The idea of rethinking an entirely new way of working is highly appealing and energizing
4. Lena feels stuck and unsatisfied in role	Exercise more creativity at work without moving to a new role. Why important? To stay engaged and productive	**Engage team members to collaborate differently and creatively**	Expand capacity to influence and build relationship with peers

Step #3: Agree on the Topic

As the coach and coachee negotiate WDW, the goal is to reach an agreement on the development goal. "Agreement on the Topic" is Step #3 of the model.

Using the analogy of having an acquaintance for lunch, imagine again sitting at a set table with the meal directly in front of you. After Step #2, your guest has changed or seasoned some of the dishes. The agreement is when the host and the guest both look at the dishes and find the meal nutritious and appetizing to eat! If not, both stay in Step #2 and find a different dish or better combination of ingredients.

Bridging from WDW to Agreement on the Topic begins by testing whether the coachee will join with you on WDW. Questions to bridge include:

- "I'm interested in your view of this."
- "Do you know what I'm talking about?"
- "Is this your experience, too?"
- "Can you see why this could be a concern?"
- "Do you see that your development in this area could help you meet your goal of...?"

In other cases, "Agreement on the Topic" may have already been established during Step #2, and the coach takes adequate time to confirm and test it. It's important to listen carefully and track whether the coachee is comfortable with the conclusions thus far and beginning to take responsibility for what they want to learn. What you need is an *explicit* agreement, a version of "Yes, this is something I want to work on." Remember that questions of hierarchy may make the coachee feel there is no choice but to agree. Refuse to move on unless you are convinced the coachee is agreeing. If the coachee hesitates even a little, point out the hesitation or ask another question about their concerns. An agreement can take several minutes or be part of a series of conversations when working to understand a foundational orientation. Gaining agreement on the developmental topic is often the most difficult part of any coaching experience because the coachee is building new awareness.

The agreed-upon topic is often a broad idea as well as a specific aspect that will be explored during this coaching session. For example, if the coachee struggles with trying very hard in everything she does (expending excessive effort at times), the broad development topic may be how to integrate more ease into the day. The coach could ask, "What part of experimenting with ease would be most helpful for us to discuss today?" The client can identify a particular context to start the exploration – a particular meeting, with a particular person or customer, etc. – where finding ease is most difficult for her.

The Arrow

Note the arrow pointing away from the model in this step. Exiting the coaching process can occur anytime, but especially at Step #3. Using the meal analogy, your guest may not agree that the main course looks or smells good and does not want to eat anything! Exiting the coaching process means that the conversation turns into advice, debate, discussion, or something else, but you will not be in a position to coach. There are many reasons this can happen, but the answer is found in prior steps of the model – insufficient trust or an unclear/uncompelling want, dilemma, or WIFM. Coaches can do many things to increase the possibilities for agreement (many already articulated), but the client has ultimate responsibility for making the choice that's right for him. This is a key mindset for a coach: *whether a client takes on the developmental dilemma is his choice*. The coach also has choices, of course, to consider the client's job-fit, suitability for role, learning orientation, etc.

TRUST AND EMPATHY IN CONTRACTING

By Rita Jókay

Certified Facilitator of Manager-as-Coach I & II

In the Manager-as-Coach workshop, I was eager to show how the Developmental Coaching Model (DCM) worked and asked a participant to help me demonstrate it. A volunteer raised the following issue: he has trouble talking loud enough. He had received a lot of feedback on this point, but his dilemma is when he raises his voice he feels a pain in his chest. That day, he was talking into a microphone because of the noisy air conditioning in the room which made him especially difficult to hear due to his soft and low voice. At the same time, the situation was strange to me and a little frustrating in my ability to feel I could establish a quality connection with him.

(Reflection: to build trust in the conversation you need to have circumstances and atmosphere which comforts both people).
We continued talking and began exploring his topic, where he said several times he needed my advice. I admit I thought he was challenging me by repeating his need for advice (when we had spent time establishing that coaches should avoid giving advice) and I realized later that his repeated request meant he wasn't yet ready for exploration of the topic.

(Reflection: an emotional tuning in with the coachee is necessary to achieve openness and sharing of vulnerabilities and weaknesses).
Eager to show how the cycle works, we moved on despite the warning signs. As we discussed, I stated my hypothesis that he had a reticence to

impact others but he was not receptive. A couple of times, I asked him what his topic might be and made suggestions, but he turned all ideas away.

(Reflection: I couldn't get agreement on the topic, even after moving to Step #4, which does sometimes help the coachee to clarify a topic.)

It became obvious we were stuck. We couldn't move further and stayed in Step #1 and Step #2, not being able to go on, as he did not feel true support from me to his issue.

I was of course puzzled of what went wrong and was curious to discuss what happened. What followed was a wonderful discussion reflecting with him and with the group and we discovered that the main point I missed as a coach was to attend to his pain, that he really suffers from this issue and he really needs full acceptance and full confirmation of how this makes his life and work difficult. I was truly sorry about that, which I shared with him and we understood that my eagerness to demonstrate the steps in this case got in my way and resulted in less empathy. I really wanted to make the discussion "learningful" for him but what he really needed was for me to truly attend to his issue.

(Reflection: Empathy is essential in coaching to support the client to bring up his issue where he is stuck.)

We shouldn't forget that bringing up any issue may cause concern that he isn't good enough or isn't performing. When we engage ourselves in a discussion, we need to have in mind how delicate each situation can be. If we want our clients to come out of their comfort zone and expose their vulnerability, we as manager-coaches need to bring our genuine warmth toward this other human being to provide an environment of trust and safety.

Challenges of Step #3

- *Reaching a pseudo-agreement.* People at times agree when they are not truly convinced of an idea. The coach needs to be on the lookout for signals (often non-verbal) that real agreement is not actually in place. In our coaching workshop, observers of coaching conversations easily pick out the "I'm-saying-yes-but-don't-really-mean-it" clients. New coaches tend to struggle to notice the signals because of their focus and motivation to reach an agreement. Clients also can be eager to please, only to realize later they are ambivalent. While not a coaching situation, a personal anecdote may provide further insight. I was asked to be part of a global team to overhaul the website for a global, consulting organization I belonged to. My first reaction to the request was, "No, not my thing, thanks." But the executive director was charming and I reasoned that the project would be developmental in some ways. Unfortunately, I soon recognized my own lack of resolve and regretted the decision. I decided to fully dedicate myself to the first phase of the project and then let the team continue without me. What a coach might have done to tie the business need to my development could have ensured a sustained effort. I had been interested in finding a forum to build more relationships with my consulting peers around the world, and this project would deliver that. But I didn't independently think through how this group could be part of my larger vision, and the project lost purpose for me.

■ *The coach has trouble getting the coachee to taste the meal.* Like having a guest for lunch who is deciding whether the meal is appetizing (will he enjoy or choke it down?), the coach tries to make the topic appetizing. The coach does want the client to engage and the coach's influence style does impact how effective she is. Consider if your coaching client likes facts, figures, or concrete reasons. Or does he prefer to imagine the future and its possibilities? Or does he love to talk ideas through with others, feeling engaged when brainstorming in a collaborative way? The coach's style also affects with whom she tends to be most effective, and being able to engage in different ways will impact one's outcomes.[7]

■ *Insufficient cultural knowledge.* Coaches should expect unfamiliar scenarios and explore them with the client. I've been a student and resource to others on the fascinating topic of cross-cultural effectiveness for 30 years. Recently, I suggested to a Chinese client that he ask for feedback from his manager, and we spent several conversations discussing the idea. He had a dilemma: In his experience, feedback is never to be requested; it's only offered when *the giver* determines the desire or need to give it. "If she had feedback for me," he explained, "she would have already given it to me. If I ask, and she feels obliged to say something when she doesn't *want* to do so, she will be put in a very difficult situation. The fact that I've *asked* her, and she doesn't *want* to do so, will forever remain as an uncomfortable part of our history." Note that the coach's goal is not to change the logic or world view. Instead, demonstrating curiosity will naturally allow for more awareness of one's own assumptions and new, expanded choices. In the case of my client, he discovered as we spoke that he could ask his manager for feedback based on his participation in our executive development program which was designed for expanded modes of learning and building more awareness.

Step #4: "How Can I Be Useful (in this conversation)?"

The question "How can I be most useful (in this conversation)?" is the last step of the Contracting phase. The question comes just after Agree on the Topic, and the coach pauses to ask about her role. The question may surprise the coachee at first because of an assumption we hold about managers – they *give advice* and *solve problems*. So why ask about role in this conversation? First, calling into question the role is intended to further dispel the assumption that it's *the manager* who's in charge of the coachee's development. Compare two possible responses:

#1
Coach: How can I be most useful to you in this conversation?
Client: Can you talk to the CFO about this issue?

#2
Coach: How can I be most useful to you in this conversation?
Client: Can you listen to what I'm planning to say to the CFO and give me your reaction?

In the first response, the coach is handed all the responsibility. The coach steps away from the temptation to provide answers because it's the coachee's *responsibility and developmental opportunity* to address it. The coach may want to clarify "I'm not planning to solve this for you, but I'm open to hear more and support you in this." The coachee may feel anxious that he won't get quick answers but this is to be expected. It's a manager's job to *challenge*, as well as support her employees.

Another purpose of Step #4 is easily described with this analogy: A friend wants your help to move into a new house. There are lots of things you *could* do – move boxes, unpack, clean shelves, entertain the kids, walk the dog, or bring lunch. It's easiest (and the best outcome for the friend) to ask what is most helpful. Asking the coachee to define the kind of support needed helps the coachee hone skills in critical thinking skills in relation to self-development. What aspect in particular about talking to the CFO is difficult? The coachee who requests a particular kind of support – a brain-stormer, listener, devil's advocate, encourager, observer, parser of ideas, role-player, etc. – has better self-awareness about where he gets stuck. From the coach's side of things, knowing what kind of help is needed makes the next step much easier.

See Table 4.2, which is a build from Table 4.1 but includes Step #4. Note that we assume that the client has *agreed* to the developmental topic (Step #3), so there isn't a separate column for it. In real life, however, the scope of the coaching topic would likely change as it's refined and shaped together with the coachee.

What Else Happens in Step #4?

■ *Help clarify Step #3.* Sometimes the agreement still seems vague or imprecise no matter how much you try to scope it in Steps #2 and 3. Moving to Step #4 will often provoke more clarity, at which point a clearer agreement will emerge. It's as if you move from Step #4, then back to #3, then on to Step #5. For example:

Coach: We've agreed that your key development right now is about staying organized when things get busy. How can I be most useful right now to support your development in this area?

Coachee: The most helpful would be to discuss how you stay calm amongst all the busyness. How do you stay focused?

Notice how the coachee takes the conversation into the direction of stay-ing focused, instead of getting organized. By asking the ques-tion, the coach has uncovered either a second developmental concern or perhaps a misunderstanding. The coach brings the question to the client right away, "which topic is more pressing and why?" or "earlier we used the word 'organized,' but just now you've said 'focused'?" The contracting continues until the pair have landed on what would be most meaningful for the coachee and what role the coach will take.

Table 4.2 Example Steps #2 – #4

Presenting Topic	The Want ... and why Step #2 (WDW)	Developmental dilemma [Agreement established - Step #3 - is depicted in bold] Step #2 (WDW)	WIFM Step #2 (WDW)	Coach's Role Step #4
1. Diana spends a lot of time on emails and meetings	Be more strategic; Spend time to reflect and act on issues critical to the business long term. Why important? Fire-fighting does not replace long-term solutions	**Manage expectations of the internal stakeholders** who send many requests for information	Be seen as an enterprise-wide thinker; become a more visionary leader	**Play devil's advocate to ensure the ideas correspond to the organizational realities**
2. Marcos feels resentful and angry at the R&D director for being so difficult to work with	Improve relationship with R&D director. Why important? Collaboration is not optional; Business results are required	**Say "no" to those who push too hard or are inflexible**	Respecting own needs (establishing boundaries) will recalibrate the relationship. Ability to manage conflict will help in all aspects of client's life.	**Role-play the conversation, with coach playing R&D director. Client gives feedback about the impact of the behavior**

(Continued)

Table 4.2 (*Continued*)   Example Steps #2 – #4

Presenting Topic	The Want ... and why (Step #2 – WDW)	Developmental dilemma [Agreement established - Step #3 - is depicted in bold] (Step #2 – WDW)	WIFM (Step #2— WDW)	Coach's Role (Step #4)
3. Janos is overloaded with customer work	Improve work-life balance through better time-management. Why important? Missed deadlines; dissatisfied customers; potential burnout	**Thinking outside the box** is challenging. Feeling of "I don't know how" to change my situation	The idea of rethinking an entirely new way of working is highly appealing and energizing	**Ask challenging questions to start thinking outside the box *right now***
4. Lena feels stuck and unsatisfied in role	Exercise more creativity at work. Why important? To stay engaged and productive	**Engage team members to collaborate differently and creatively**	Expand capacity to influence and build relationship with peers	**Engage on topic of how to engage team members using the principles of creative thinking by not shooting down any idea, and being expansive**

■ *Address lingering concerns about the agreed-upon topic.* Before moving to Phase III, Step #4 also presents the opportunity to address ancillary and related items that are unfinished and distracting: Is there a lingering concern about the topic in your mind or the coachee's ownership of the topic? Did something mentioned earlier in the conversation go unaddressed?

In a recent coaching case, I had a lingering concern with the agreed-upon topic. As we moved into Step #4, I suspected the topic was too narrow and tactical. I also suspected I needed to probe further about what competing want, if any, was at play. Step #4, then, becomes a moment to look back at the Agreement to check scope, meaningfulness, and priority level for the client.

■ *Address any concerns about the external environment for moving into the next phase of coaching.* Examples include:

– *Safe environment.* Do both of you feel comfortable in the current space and have enough privacy to continue the conversation?

– *Time constraints.* Are you both aware of how much time you each can dedicate for the next steps of this conversation?

– *Interruptions.* Is there anything urgent that might interrupt this conversation or cut it short? Are you shutting off your phone or will you need to check it because of an urgency?

Challenges of Step #4

■ *The most common misunderstanding in Step #4 is to assume it means "How can I step in and help you resolve this?"* Instead, a coach helps the coachee to heighten awareness of *thoughts and feelings about the topic*: uncovering assumptions and biases which will meanwhile expand the coachee's breadth of choices. This is not to say it's never appropriate to lend a hand with an idea or two, but if really needed the coach's ideas can be revealed in Phase III.

■ *The coach works too hard.* We challenge coaches to listen carefully, be present, follow the model, respond authentically, and encourage clients to share. That is already a lot! Coaches who try to figure everything out – untangle the situation entirely, diagnose, brainstorm, etc. – are likely working too hard. As soon as possible in the conversation, coaches hand the thinking to the client. Remember that clients know themselves and their situation much better than the coach does. Simply asking the client to describe the support they need in Step #4 is a good example of not working too hard.

I find it useful how the coaching model helps me remember the important steps of negotiating a working contract with my client. Especially the step to clearly define the role of the coach for each specific coaching conversation. In that way both parties have an agreement about what to expect from each other and how the coach can support the client in the best way. Since support is the general idea of any coaching session, I appreciate the way the Developmental Coaching Model facilitates this.

Peter Skoglund
Certified Facilitator of workshops Manager-as-Coach I and II

Coach-Led Contracting (Steps #1–4)

In this example, more time is taken to introduce the topic and to probe about the client's willingness to engage in a developmental conversation.

Coach: Hi Sara. Thanks for coming to speak with me. Do you have 30 minutes to discuss a topic? It's related to the issue you brought up in the meeting today and I'd like to talk about a possible developmental opportunity it presents. Are you interested in discussing this?

Sara: Sure.

(The coach invites the person to sit, signaling he wants to take time for a thoughtful discussion.)

Coach: I found myself appreciating again today how you approach your tasks with so much positive energy, which is a great way to be. It reflects how much you care. You usually get excellent results whenever you pour your energy into a project. (Coach checks if Sara agrees with the assessment about her energy.) I also find myself thinking about the personal cost to you of consistently devoting so much energy into everything you do, especially when the topic is not a primary focus for you in your role. Today's meeting topic was not a primary area of focus for you, but you extended yourself considerably to achieve the goal. I imagine it must be tiring. **(Client nods ...then a short discussion on this point...)** I would like you to be more intentional about which initiatives get your time and energy **(want)**. My theory from observing you is that you give 100% effort to everything you touch, which is admirable but doesn't account for the fact that energy is finite each day! Do you agree with my comments and, if so, why is this the case? ***(…asks client to identify the dilemma…)*** Could understanding this help you achieve your goal of being less stressed and more effective at work? ***(WIFM)***

Sara: I agree I'm giving too much of myself and exhausted. But I'm not sure how to do things only partially. It's not my approach to life. If someone asks me to do something, I tackle it. I'm a team player. ***(dilemma)***

Coach: So your dilemma is to be a team player and also reserve more energy for yourself? ***(dilemma)***

Sara: Yes, but how do I *partially* respond to others or *partially* complete my tasks?

Coach: Before we go to solutions, let me ask you what reserving more energy for yourself would do for you? How would this really benefit you? ***(WIFM)***

Sara: Sometimes I get so tired. I care so much about most things I'm a part of which is emotionally exhausting. But I can't imagine setting a goal to do things only partially!

(Coach notices strong language "so tired" and "exhausting" and asks about how it feels when giving energy she doesn't have, driving the communication to a deeper place and helping the coachee raise her self-awareness. After some minutes of discussion, coach feels Sara is becoming clear.)

Coach: Do you believe that looking at how you distribute your energy could still allow you to be seen as a team player, improve outcomes, and potentially help you feel less tired? (…yes…). ***(WIFM)*** And, if so, is this something you want to work on? ***(Agree on the Topic)***

Sara: Yes, and yes!

Coach: What do you think about playing with the idea of how – and in what contexts – you might give different amounts of energy? How does that sound as a place to start today? (…) ***(Agreement on the Topic, further scoped)***

Sara: Yes, I like the idea.

Coach: OK. How can I be most useful to you as we discuss this? ***(How can I be most useful in this conversation?)***

Sara: Maybe I can start to identify which things I'm spending a lot of energy and time doing that don't correspond to my annual goals.

(Agreement on the Topic, modified again by discussing Step #4) Can you point out anything I'm prioritizing that you disagree with?
(Coach notices the shift in topic and that Sara has started to lead. The coach follows Sara's lead.

Coach: Sounds interesting. Linking annual goals with how we spend our day is not as easy as it seems but is really important. So yes, I'll point out anything that seems at odds. And … before we go forward, I'm aware people are starting to walk by and I feel distracted. It's also no longer quiet or confidential here. Would you like to move to the conference room?

Step #4, then, aims to reset expectations for both coach and coachee, gently transferring to the client control of the conversation and ownership of her own learning and development. At the same time, the coach has learned more about the coachee, encouraged her, and built more trust.

Client-Led Contracting (Steps #2, #3, and #4)

> Everything is energy and that's all there is to it. Match the frequency of the reality you want, and you cannot help but get that reality. It can be no other way.
>
> **— Albert Einstein**

Client-led coaching is one that the client initiates. The topic was their idea. (The coach, however, is still responsible to take the lead role of guiding using the DCM.) The topic might be career-related, job-related, skill-related, or even what's going on outside of work. *Like coach-led coaching, the desired outcome of client-led contracting is a coachee who has examined one or more of his assumptions, raised self-awareness, taken ownership of a developmental topic, and is highly interested to experiment with new ideas and behaviors in relation to his effectiveness.*

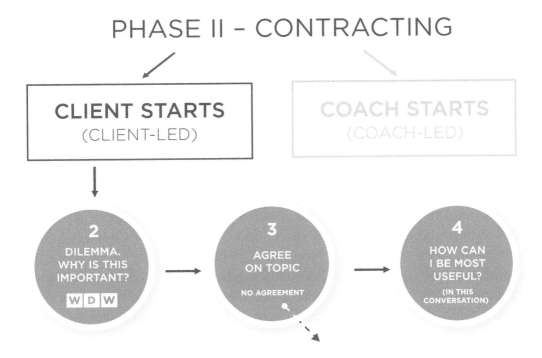

It's important to note that when the client brings up a topic, being coached may or may not be his goal. To avoid incorrect assumptions and potential erosion of trust, explicitly asking the question is useful as part of the contracting process. This can be done in many ways; one is, "Would you like to explore this topic together, in a coaching kind of way? I'm happy to listen and support."

Like coach-led situations, the conversation might be a planned, sit-down conversation, or be impromptu, but no matter who begins the conversation, the coach is still guiding the coaching process. The same steps in the model apply, with a few considerations:

- (Step #1) Adequate trust is still a prerequisite. One could argue that trust is likely in place already because the coachee is looking for input from the manager-coach in the first place, unsolicited. Nonetheless, the coach doesn't take this for granted and looks to establish more trust in the moment.
- (Steps #2, #3) The coach listens for each element of WDW. Very often one or more elements will be missing. As with coach-led coaching, explore deeply the WIFM. Explicitly agree on the topic for the coaching.
- (Step #4) The coach asks how she can be useful in the conversation to support the client's development.
- (Steps #5- 7) The coach guides in the same way as coach-led coaching. (These steps will be covered in the next chapter.)

What's Different about Client-Led Coaching

In addition to the caveats above, there are several other considerations for client-led coaching.

Client-Led Coaching Opportunities Are Often Camouflaged

Opportunities to coach come in many shapes and sizes. A statement or question from the client might be direct and clear, such as "I need help to prioritize all of these requests." More often, what's said may be more casual and indirect: "My direct report doesn't delegate well," or "I'm not sure how we'll manage this." For these kinds of statements, the coach needs to be listening with "developmental ears," become interested in the statement, and test whether there is an opportunity to coach.

Below is a self-awareness assessment to test your leadership habits. Look at the four statements below, and ask yourself whether the client's statement or question is either a direct or indirect coaching opportunity. Then, ask yourself how you would most likely respond: With a *problem-solving approach*? Or *engaging further* with the intent to engage, learn, and potentially coach?

**SELF-AWARENESS: PROBLEM SOLVE OR
SHIFT TO ENGAGE AND LEARN?**

#1: Client asks: "How can I influence her?"	
(Response: problem-solving) "You know you'll need to get on better terms with her."	(Response: engage and learn) "Influence is an important topic in your role … Tell me about your past experience trying to influence her."
#2: Client says: "My direct report doesn't delegate well."	
(Response: problem-solving) "I suggest you make delegation part of his performance improvement plan."	(Response: engage and learn) "Delegation is a critical skillset for managers, but not easy to learn, especially for a first-time manager. Have you been working with him on this topic?"
#3: Client says: "I'm not sure how we'll manage this complex situation."	
(Response: problem-solving) "First, you'll need to talk to procurement."	(Response: engage and learn) "Yes, there are a lot of parts to this situation. How are you thinking it through?"
#4: Client says: "I might be ready for an opportunity like that."	
(Response: problem-solving) "Yes, I think you are ready." (or "I'm not sure you're ready yet because …")	(Response: engage and learn) "Tell me more about what you are looking for in that opportunity."

The more camouflaged (indirect) coaching opportunities are the last three. Which response did you find more familiar – solving problems or engaging to learn more? If your instinct was to provide solutions, here's the issue: while you are likely a very good problem-solver, it's not *your* puzzle, and it does not help your coachee to solve *his* puzzle. Instead, as you listen, ask yourself: "Why is this person telling me this?" and "Is this topic a learning opportunity?" To find out, the coach engages and gathers more information:

■ "Say more about that."
■ "What are the implications of this issue for you?"

- "What are your thoughts about that?"
- "What do you foresee as interesting/challenging/the learning for you in this?"

As in coach-led, the coach is showing interest, tuning in, getting baseline information, and working to understand. Then, she moves to the first part of WDW: *Convert what's said into a clear, positive statement of what the coachee wants, such as* "Interesting statement. It sounds like you would like to have empathy for your direct reports," versus responding with a solution, such as "To stop being so critical of others means you need to stop being so critical of yourself."

WHAT'S WRONG WITH BEING A PROBLEM-SOLVER?

There's nothing wrong with problem-solving in and of itself. When situations are urgent, problem-solving may be exactly what's needed. But when managers rely too much on this mode, they commonly are (1) serving their own need (often unconsciously) to be the hero, the designated thinker, the one in control, and/or (2) prioritizing speed over development, at high cost to the organization. The satisfaction and gains of problem-solving are reversed when considering the losses of learning and development over time. Ironically, the manager also may be working against her own best interests: People respect leaders who empower *them* to be the designated thinker.

Client-Led Coaching Opportunities Come at Inconvenient Moments

Client-led coaching topics are rarely presented at the perfect time for the coach when there is adequate time. In fact, this is a major challenge of client-led coaching: it's hard to squeeze in a meaningful conversation with so much else going on unless the client has brought it to a prearranged meeting dedicated to it. As such, the coach must make a choice: Shape the present moment to make time, or follow up later. For example:

Adrian: I don't like these kinds of situations we get ourselves into.
Coach: Interesting statement, Adrian. Briefly, what do you mean by that?
I'd like to understand your thinking." (…) *Then (if the comment is deemed possibly developmental), the coach could add* "Let's take 15 minutes to discuss this point, if you are interested" *or* "At our

next one-on-one, I'd like to talk about this point again because I see it could be a learning opportunity. What do you think?"

Never underestimate your ability to support a coaching client based on the duration of time. Effective coaching can occur in less than 10 minutes. It's a matter of scoping and raising his/her awareness for a new or expanding area of focus. Remember, the work belongs to the client and his/her pacing.

Harold Hill
Certified Facilitator of the Workshops, Manager-as-Coach I and II

How Does Client-Led Contracting Sound? (Steps #1-4)

Below is an example of a client-led coaching case. See which differences you detect from a coach-led coaching scenario.

Sergei: *(Walks into manager's office, standing just inside the door.)* You should know our customer is unhappy with the product we shipped this week, and I've tried everything to appease her.

Coach: Hi Sergei. Thanks for letting me know. Tell me a little more about the situation. (***Step #1 - Establish a climate of Trust; gathering information***)

Sergei: The product originally shipped late because we couldn't get a sign-off from Quality. Then we shipped it out as a rush order and then they claimed it didn't meet their specifications. I showed them that it did match using the proof documents, but they are still not backing down. They want a full refund or a replacement within a month. Replacement will be impossible because engineering is underwater on work right now.

Coach: I understand. You mentioned trying to appease her? (*turns the focus to the coachee, moving toward the want; gathering information*)

Sergei: Yes, I said we eventually could get her a replacement but we need more time and a new contract for the rework. She's not happy with that. I told her I'd find out if there was anything else we could do, which is why I'm here talking to you. (*Asks for help with problem-solving*)

Coach: (*Coach sees the development opportunity and starts with Step #1*). This is an unfortunate situation and I can see you're concerned. I'm sure you are eager to find a reasonable resolution, plus help the customer. (***Step #1 – Trust*** *using empathy*) What would you like to have happen, given this situation? (***Step #2 – business want***)

Sergei: I'm frustrated. I want Quality to be on time with their inspections and for our clients to stand by their agreements with us. (***Step #2 – business wants***)

Coach: Of those two issues, which seems more important in this scenario? (*Coaching wisdom: Only take on one topic at a time. Ask client to select between any options that emerge. As a default, pick the one that seems bigger or has more implications for the situation and person.*)

Sergei: Clients who stand by their agreements is the most critical, because even if we would have delivered the product on time, we'd still be in the situation where the client is not accepting the product. (***business want***)

Coach: OK, you're here to talk about this customer, but first, I'd like to take a few minutes to talk about what's underneath this issue and what this means for your own learning. Can you take 15 minutes right now to have a coaching conversation? (***Step #1 – Trust*** *and transitioning from problem-solving to coaching*)
(*Assuming a "yes" response, the coach continues. If the timing is not adequate, schedule time to discuss development in the near future.*)

Coach: (*Coach invites the person to sit, to signal taking time for a thoughtful discussion.*) You said you wanted customers that keep their commitments. What is it that you want for yourself – to have in your own abilities and skillsets – as it relates to this? (***Step #2 –*** *Probing for a* ***personal want***)

Sergei: We don't do a good job of making sure the right person on the customer side is signing off of the product specs. Probably the person I'm working with didn't understand what she was signing off on. (*Sergei deflects without accepting personal responsibility.*)

Coach: Interesting. Say more … (*Supporting the client to reflect further*)

Sergei: Well, based on my past experience, people there have poor communication and are moving too fast. So, they sign off and then go back on the agreement later.

Coach: I see. Anything else? (*Supporting the client to reflect, again, with a joining statement*)

Sergei: I probably need to ask more questions about who has seen the specs and the implications of the requirements being wrong. (Coach notices that Sergei took some responsibility here.)

Coach: That's a good insight. Let's stay with that line of thinking. Can you expand on that? (**Step #2** – *more about the personal want*)

Sergei: Well, she's really busy, and she has demanding internal customers, while I'm under constant pressure to get the drawings to engineering. I can see it's a bad combination.

Coach: What you are saying also tracks with my experience of you. In my view, you very much want to have alignment with internal and external customers, and you also like to move fast, to be responsive and efficient. You want two things, both of which are admirable but can conflict. Is that a fair assessment? (**developmental dilemma**, *broadening the issue to a pattern.*)

Sergei: There is never time to get everything done. Clearly in this case, I needed more alignment.

Coach: It seems you realize there are times to be fast and times to slow it down. I imagine you'd feel good about spending more time on certain tasks to reduce the risk of losing alignment. Is becoming more aware of your speed something you want to do? (**Agree on the Topic**) And if so, in what ways could that help you? (**WIFM**)

Sergei: Yes, because as we see today, I'm not actually saving myself any time! (**WIFM**)

Coach: Say more about that. (*Coach wants Sergei to engage more deeply on the topic and the benefit of taking action.*)

Sergei: But how do I slow down when everything is always so urgent? How do *you* do it? (*Changing the topic to prioritization. And trying to move to problem-solving or advice … Coach doesn't fall for it!*)

Coach: Let's hold on going to solutions, because if you understand yourself better, next steps will come easily. First, what do you think about reflecting on your patterns of pace, along with some examples. (*The coach stays on track, wanting to get a clear* **WDW** *and* **Agreement on the Topic – Step #3**)

Sergei: Yes, this could help. It's like I have two speeds: high and *off*!

Coach: (*Continues learning about Sergei through extended probing based on his last comment.*) It's not easy to break a habit like moving fast. But moving fast cuts your awareness about many things around you. I would say that your #1 job is being acutely aware of your situations, the people around you, and yourself (feelings, needs), so that you can make good decisions.

Sergei: Becoming more aware of my speed and its impact seems important, although I'm not sure what it really means in practice.

Coach: OK, shall we agree that we'll begin by discussing what awareness means in practice, beginning with the topic of speed? *(**Step #3 – Agree on the topic**)*

Sergei: Yes, I think so. I'm motivated. This seems like a blind spot because I know I miss important information at times. *(**Step #3 – Agree on the topic**, **WIFM**)*

Coach: Do you want to discuss this now, and if so, how can I be most useful as you talk this through? *(**Step #4 – How can I be most useful in this conversation?**)*

Sergei: I'd like to do some thinking and then come back to you on this.

Coach: Sounds good. When should we follow up? (…) How do you feel about our conversation thus far? (…) *The coach jumps over Steps #5 and 6 for now, and gathers important feedback - Step #7. We'll see these steps in the next chapter. Progress has been made in identifying a development need. Coaching is resumed after allowing time for reflection.)*

Coach: Now, what are your thoughts about next steps about our unhappy customer? *(Coach asks coachee's ideas about what could appease the client. This is a problem-solving exercise, but using the coachee's brain instead of the coach's. The coachee is surely also thinking about at what speed the approach requires!)*

Sergei's Case: Further Analysis

Sergei's question "What should I do to appease the customer?" is direct, straightforward, and highly coachable (although many managers have developed the habit of actually *answering* these kinds of questions). *This is the shift that many managers miss completely. Instead, they simply respond to the business topic presented to them by giving advice or approving the decision, such as* "OK, give them a refund … or negotiate … etc." This is a non-coaching response. Note how the coach slows Sergei down and takes plenty of time to contract. Your patience through this phase builds understanding, relationship, learning, and commitment. It's time well spent.

Notice, also, we've given a peek at **Step #7**, "Summarize. How do you feel. Was this useful?" We'll cover this part of the model in the next chapter, but it's important to realize that conversations can conclude at the end of the contracting phase. While coaching has two parts, identifying the developmental topic and then working the issue, in this case, Sergei and his coach pause after Step #3 to allow the coachee to further consider the agreed upon topic.

Contracting Wisdoms

We conclude this chapter with three wisdoms about contracting which tightly correspond to a coaching mindset. In fact, the first is one we've seen before, but we look at it again given its centrality to the Contracting phase.

Wisdom #1: See Resistance As Natural and Necessary

Resistance to feedback, which is naturally part of coach-led coaching, is common because humans are hard-wired to feel threatened and stay "alive." When managers of people (or parents or governments, for that matter) impose themselves in a way perceived as threatening, the reaction of upset or rebellion should be expected. Of course, those who resist are characterized as not having understood or appreciated the benefits that the change offers. (Note that managers also resist being resisted.) Resistance includes deflecting, denying, quick acceptance without considering, blaming (self or others), or appeasing. These are forms of self-protection. And yet, if resistance is a lock, it's also the key! Without resistance, we, humans, would go along with everything we came across. All suggestions and recommendations would be taken up. People would be order-takers. By consequence, our own lived experience and reality would be denied and result in a loss of our own identities.

Learning to embrace the resistance you feel from others is the path to easing the stress which comes from anticipating different perspectives. Easing one's need to control the situation is part of the art of coach-led coaching (and maybe happiness in life, for that matter). To "solve" the conundrum of seeing things as true or false, consider that different perspectives can be true at the same time. This is the purpose of articulating a dilemma, with both perspectives at play and both framed in a positive way. The coach and coachee are embracing multiple realities, including that two or more things must be managed. By not making one person wrong, resistance dissipates. In practice, people are at least 1% ambivalent on any topic (even if they don't recognize it), and this presents the opportunity to learn more about that part.

Wisdom #2: Be Transparent

Manager-coaches often hold many thoughts and feelings impacting their nervous system before and during coaching conversations. Some hold their appreciation and emotions. Some hold difficult topics and concerns. Holding back leads to more complication.

COACHES WORRY ...

Coaches Worry ...	Then ...	Result
... about not being able to manage the emotion that could emerge (their own or the coachee's)	... waiting increases the anxiety further. The coach continues to put off the topic, hoping the situation will somehow resolve itself	Coach finally talks to coachee but then does so with pent-up frustration, resulting in an emotionally charged moment
... about upsetting the coachee which will in turn put the business goals at risk	... the coach thinks about ways the coachee could fix the situation, becomes attached to her ideas, preventing the coachee from coming up with his own solution	The coachee perceives the coach's anxiousness and desire to control and impose ideas. The coachee becomes fearful and defensive, and rejects the coaching

While expressing the topic, *be transparent about these feelings and thoughts*. Introduce a topic in two parts: (1) Relay the problem, and (2) say how you are feeling about it right now. For example, "This is a problem we need to address. I realize I've been slow to bring this up. I've been part of the problem. I've not brought it up because I realize I'm afraid you'll reject any new ideas and this could create a conflict between us." By *telling* the person openly why *you* are also part of this issue, trust is reinforced and the possibility for agreement expands. Transparency begets trust because the coach takes her rightful share of the responsibility, shares something deeper about herself, and encourages the coachee to do the same.

Wisdom #3: Be Highly Attentive to Power Dynamics

It would be naïve to ignore the topic of power dynamics and the obvious differential between manager and coachee. The manager is situated in an organizational power structure and, as such, is in a position of advantage. Managers are also not solely dedicated to the coachee, but also beholden to the organization (and themselves). There is no need for negative attribution regarding these realities: Individuals with organizational power are of critical importance to support a closer alignment within the organization. Hierarchies are, indeed, meant to provide resolution of conflicts among many stakeholder interests.

Interestingly, managers sometimes deny entirely the very existence of a power differential: "I'm just one of the guys/girls." While some might prefer to downplay or refute the realities of the hierarchical structure (the sentiment is perhaps noble), the reality of the disequilibrium remains.

When we prescribe the language of WDW, we aim to counteract some of these forces. With the language of "I want …" our intention is to create alignment between the coach's need and their speech. (Ritualistic statements such as "I would appreciate if you …," which sometimes means "you must do this," can confuse and impede the possibility for authentic exchange.[8]) Challenge yourself to be authentic in your language. Likewise, the language of "theory" is meant to create open exchange and deepen the conversation, while assuming the coach can remember that the responsibility for self-actualization and development truly is the decision of the coachee.

IS THE COACHEE ACTUALLY RESPONSIBLE FOR THIS ISSUE?

Managers who acknowledge their own behavior and the organization's role in impacting individuals sees the entire organizational system for what it is: a set of interrelated dynamics and dependencies. Recognizing this fact gives managers more choices based on mutual accountabilities, instead of acting in ways that put the burden exclusively on employees to figure it out.

Managers must ask themselves about their own role – and the organization's role – in creating the situations we look to employees to solve.

Manager-coaches can unfairly put too much responsibility on their coachees to adjust and adapt, when the organization may need to make adjustments (for example) in clearer goals, roles, or processes. Manager-coaches can ask themselves:

■ Have I/has the organization set an environment that explains the choices the coachee is making? If so, how will I acknowledge it and take responsibility, too?

■ Have I/has the organization rewarded the coachee in such a way to foresee this result? If so, how will I acknowledge it and take responsibility, too?

■ Do I/does the organization assign resources in ways that could predict this behavior? If so, how will I acknowledge it and take responsibility, too?

When the Coachee Is a Peer or Manager

As mentioned in Chapter 2, for reasons of hierarchy and power, coaching a direct report is considered more straightforward than coaching one's peers or manager. It's the role of a people manager to help develop her team, after all, and to be supported and developed is also the direct report's hope and expectation. To coach a peer or manager, consider the following key differences (Figure 4.2).

Remember that if the motivation to coach a peer or manager is to convince him or her of something they seem unwilling or unable to do, this is a question of influencing, not coaching. Coaching is meant to support a person to grow in the direction that *he/she* sees as motivating. The coach's stance must be of absolute service to the other's interests. To coach a peer or manager, therefore, tends to necessitate very high curiosity and an altruistic, personal investment of time and energy.

When the Coachee Is a Peer

The unspoken assumption in most organizations is that developmental support comes from one's immediate manager only. There is typically no organizational expectation or structure for peers to coach one other. (The closest practice to coaching may be 360-degree feedback from peers, usually done

Coaching a Direct Report		Coaching a Peer or Manager
Power	Coach	Coachee
Trust	Implied in the relationship (although never taken for granted)	Needs to be established first (and with explicit permission)
Data	Coach has more behavioral data due to a closer working relationship (but also more bias?)	Coach will need more data points given less exposure to other aspects of the person's work and life
Goal	Guidance and encouragement to maximize coachee's potential	

Figure 4.2   Key differences between coaching direct reports versus peers or one's manager.

via electronic survey and anonymously.) A trusting working relationship or friendship can result in coaching between peers, but this tends to be rare.

Luckily, coaching a peer doesn't have to be nearly as infrequent as it is. Doing so requires a willingness to go against the grain of normal organizational behavior, and requires good contracting skills. Quite frequently, resistance to being coached involves the ego: Is the offer felt as one peer asserting power over the other? As such, peer-to-peer coaching needs effective contracting to flatten any accompanying power differential that may be triggered. Doing so can happen in numerous ways, and in combination, for example:

- Ask permission. For example, "I'd like to be helpful to you on this topic. Would you be interested in my coaching you on this? I don't have the answers, but I could perhaps help you talk it through." Notice in this example that the coach is also setting expectations about what constitutes coaching, versus problem-solving or advice-giving.
- Share why you are interested to coach him/her. For example, "I'd like to help you with a coaching conversation, if you're interested. After all, you've helped me in similar ways."

■ Ask to be coached first. For example, "Would you be willing to coach me on a topic that I'm struggling with? I'm not looking for you to solve my issue, but to ask me questions that help me get clear what I want, what I want to get better at, and maybe how to work on it." Again, note that the coach sets expectations about what coaching really is. After being coached, ask if the peer is interested to become peer coaches for each other, with coaching going both directions.

All of the above could be considered a preliminary layer of contracting about the relationship, before the contracting on the topic.

When the Coachee Is the Manager

As with offering to coach a peer, the first two phases of the DCM are often handled more deliberately with a manager given the dynamics, power structures, and the associated perception of risk.

The same strategies from the above section still apply. When permissioning, even if the manager agrees to being coached, remember that the manager may feel obligated given that leaders have typically been told hundreds of times during their careers that they must be open and receptive to others, even if they are not really open and receptive. Ways to double-check openness and receptivity could include:

■ Relaying the interest to coach while acknowledging that it's unconventional
■ Explaining what you have in mind and why (i.e., the topic, how it could be useful, why you are suggesting coaching at all, how it connects to who you are as a leader, etc.)
■ Including a discussion with the manager about the pros and cons of starting two-way coaching conversations, including any feelings you have in doing so
■ Assuming a "yes" response, suggesting a time in the near future to have the coaching conversation, instead of in that moment, noticing if she follows up or refers to the agreement again

These discussions have value in their own right, while also giving the manager time to interrogate herself about her own openness or resistance to the idea. A manager who quickly agrees to be coached could be doing so as a defense. Keep the conversation deliberate and slow to build trust and alignment.

It's a shame more coaching upward doesn't take place, why learning cannot take priority over issues of ego, fear, and vulnerability. At the same time, there is no need to overcomplicate the dynamic – sometimes coaching upwards is accepted easily, just requiring some leadership courage to bring it up.

Final Comments on Contracting

You've made it through the topic of Contracting – and hopefully experimenting along the way – resisting the urge, again and again, to jump into problem-solving mode, to control the person or situation, or to make undue assumptions that undermine engagement. These will tempt you, requiring leadership discipline and maturity. Understanding that the early phases of coaching involve navigating fissures in trust, past discord, internal anxieties, and fears about conflict is enough to send some managers believing it's all too much.

And yet, with the challenge comes the payoff: coaches learn to engage, build trust, develop others, and solve business issues, all at the same time. Successfully doing so comes with enormous satisfaction. It's quite common for clients to feel a positive, emotional release, or an "aha" moment, when they recognize something new about themselves. Sensing they're no longer "stuck," a kind of euphoria springs forth from the new insight. Coaches can also take pleasure in being a part of that discovery.

It may be an ideal time to pause and stay in awareness – for a few minutes or a few weeks – but coaches know that coaching has two distinct parts: to identify a developmental dilemma of importance to the coachee, and then to address it. In the next chapter, the coach supports action.

Notes

1 Argyris, Chris; Schön, Donald (1974). *Theory in Practice*. Increasing professional effectiveness. San Francisco, CA: Jossey-Bass.
2 It's also plausible that upon further probing about Julian's pattern, Julian could reflect further about his propensity to maintain harmony that he regularly says "Yes" when he means "No," or perhaps that he even dislikes working in his external customer-facing role!
3 Bridges, W. (2009). *Managing Transitions: Making the Most of Change*. Cambridge, MA: Da Capo Press.

4 Corporate Leadership Council. (2004). Driving performance and retention through employee engagement. Retrieved from https://www.stcloudstate.edu/humanresources/_files/documents/supv-brown-bag/employee-engagement.pdf.

5 IBID.

6 Davret, B. (2020). How to make someone feel extraordinary by saying very little. *Medium*. Retrieved from https://medium.com/swlh/how-to-make-someone-feel-extraordinary-by-saying-very-little-887811246bae. Accessed 1/5/2020.

7 In our Manager-as-Coach I workshop, we teach influence styles to correspond with coaching skills for this reason.

8 Moch, M., & Huff, A. S. (1983). Power enactment through language and ritual. *Journal of Business Research, 11*(3), 293–316.

Chapter 5

Phase III: Work the Idea/Issue

Taking a new step, uttering a new word is what people fear most.

— **Fyodor Dostoyevski**

With alignment intact between coach and client on the developmental topic, the coach now guides the conversation into more familiar territory: actioning. Phase III, "Work the Idea/Issue," is generally more straightforward from a process perspective because organizations (especially in the West) tend to optimize for quick, forward movement (versus reflection and long-term thinking) in the pursuit of their goals. As such, many managers tend to be more practiced, comfortable, and skilled in this realm.

It's worth repeating that sometimes novice coaches forget altogether to continue on to Phase III. Their preparation and focus on contracting have been so momentous in Phase II, that once agreement on the topic is reached, they close the conversation! Coaches shouldn't forget that coaching has two distinct parts: to *identify* and then *to address* the developmental dilemma. The coach or coachee may want to pause the process (to allow for more fully "taking in" what has been identified for further reflection), but converting the dilemma into tangible experiments and action is the intent of Phase III.

Clients gather their energy for the final, three steps in the model:

1. The client brainstorms ideas in relation to the agreed-upon development (Step #5).
2. The coach provides input, if necessary (Step #6).
3. The coach and client reflect on the conversation itself (Step #7).

Step #5: Prompt the Client to Find Solutions

In this first step of Phase III, the client explores ideas aloud with the coach on what experiments or actions will help him build more awareness about – and address – the desired development. The creative thinking comes from the client's brain, supported by the coach's questions and encouragement, but it's the coach who launches a transition question as she moves the coachee into Step #5.

Transition Questions

A "transition question" is one which ties together what's already been established in Phase II with the process of ideation. The coach's ability to listen carefully and be highly curious is critical; the coach's brain need not be racing ahead to solve anything. Instead, the coach puts herself in the coachee's shoes and wonders right along with the coachee about which experiments or actions are indicated.

There are no "correct" transition questions. Transition questions can be very simple. Three categories of sample questions follow:

1. Questions to remind clients to tap into their own wisdom
   - What were you thinking of doing?
   - What ideas do you already have about this?
   - What has worked for you in the past?
   - What do you know *doesn't* work?
2. Questions to tap into adjacent areas of knowledge
   - Do you have any experience on this topic in other contexts?
   - What advice would you give someone who asked you the same question?
   - If you had to guess how to approach this, what would you do?
3. Questions to remind them of other resources they have (or missing resources)
   - Who else have you talked to about this? What did they suggest?
   - What were the best ideas you heard?
   - Where might you start to find the answer to your question?
   - Is this a situation where you need more information before you can begin to solve? What information would be important to have?

In Table 5.1, you'll find five examples of transition questions in the last column that correspond to the cases seen in the Contracting chapter. You'll notice both simple and more synthesized transition questions. In the first example about Julian, the strategic account manager, you'll notice that the first two transition questions link his dilemma with other aspects of the discussion (the presenting issue in the first question and the WIFM in the second question).

As you read through the examples, imagine how the conversation might have evolved. The columns are written in shorthand, boiled down versions of longer conversations. The point is not to agree or disagree with the client's thinking based on the sketches provided. Each case is a set of ingredients that have become unique dishes for each coachee. Note also, that for practical purposes, we presuppose that the client agrees with the Dilemma, and hence there is no separate column for Step #3. *The sentence in bold is considered the agreed-upon topic. In practice, of course, the Dilemma would be shaped and scoped with the client before agreement happens.*

Active Listening

Skilled listening dramatically increases the odds of positive outcomes. Ironically, listening sounds simple – don't we all listen actively, or at least to the extent the content grabs our attention? Unfortunately, in fast-paced business settings, many people regularly filter out much of what they hear. They let key moments slide by.

Active listening is an advanced communication skill, whereby the listener concentrates fully on what is being said rather than passive "hearing." Active listening, involving all the senses, results in coachees who feel the freedom to talk at length and hear an audible response. In a study done in Japan which confirmed positive outcomes of active listening (96% of managers evaluated active listening training as "very meaningful" or "meaningful"), managers were asked to follow three conditions as they engaged: (1) They should not keep asking one question after another; (2) they should not change the topic chosen by the speaker; (3) they should not give advice.[1]

Other demonstrations of active listening include paraphrasing (reflecting comments back with different words), reframing (providing an alternate meaning to the coachee's experience), paralanguage (voice quality and volume), reflecting body language (demonstrating you're paying attention), emotional responses (demonstrating awareness of the emotional dimension for coachee, organization, society), and creating rapport (confirming mutual understanding).[2]

Table 5.1   Examples for Steps #1–#5

Presenting Topic	Want (and Why)	Developmental Dilemma (Step #3 Agreement Is Assumed)	WIFM	How Can I Be Most Useful (in this conversation)?	Prompt Coachee to Find Solutions
	Step #2 (WDW)	Step #2 (WDW)	Step #2 (WDW)	Step #4	Step #5
1. Julian is unable to appease Customer Jane.	Manager wants Julian to provide a consistent experience to customers. Why is this important? (1) Happy customers will forgive occasional mistakes and (2) will be more loyal to the brand; (3) Julian becomes a multifaceted resource to the customer.	Julian struggles with how to create an experience, in part because he has trouble thinking of things to talk to them about. **He wants to become more curious.** He has a bias for working with his internal customers who have come to know and respect him over time.	By engaging more with the external customer, Julian could gain insights and pass on helpful information to his internal customers.	Listen to Julian's ideas and provide a reaction; role model what curiosity looks like within this conversation.	**"What could you do to increase your level of curiosity about Customer Jane?"** or ... **"What do you think your internal customers would like to know about Customer Jane?"**

(Continued)

Table 5.1 (*Continued*)   Examples for Steps #1–#5

Presenting Topic	Want (and Why) Step #2 (W<u>D</u>W)	Developmental Dilemma (Step #3 Agreement Is Assumed) Step #2 (W<u>D</u>W)	WIFM Step #2 (WD<u>W</u>)	How Can I Be Most Useful (in this conversation)? Step #4	Prompt Coachee to Find Solutions Step #5
2. Diana spends a lot of time on emails and meetings.	Be more strategic; Spend time to reflect and act on issues critical to the business long term. Why is this important? Fire-fighting does not replace long-term solutions.	**Manage expectations of the internal stakeholders** who send many requests for information.	Be seen as an enterprise-wide thinker; become a more visionary leader.	Play devil's advocate to ensure the ideas correspond to the organizational realities.	**"Have you successfully been able to reshape someone's expectations of you in the past? What did you learn?"** **"How can you reshape others' expectations of you to allow time for more strategic initiatives?"**
3. Marcos feels resentful and angry at the R&D director for being so difficult to work with.	Improve relationship with R&D director Why is this important? Collaboration is not optional; Business results are required.	**Say "no" to those who push too hard or are inflexible.**	Respecting own needs (establishing boundaries) will recalibrate the relationship. Ability to manage conflict will help in all aspects of client's life.	Role-play the conversation, with coach playing R&D director. Client gives feedback about the impact of the behavior.	**"What did you become aware of as we role-played that conversation?"** **"How are you thinking about this now?"**

(Continued)

Table 5.1 (Continued) Examples for Steps #1–#5

Presenting Topic	Want (and Why) Step #2 (W<u>D</u>W)	Developmental Dilemma (Step #3 Agreement Is Assumed) Step #2 (W<u>D</u>W)	WIFM Step #2 (W<u>D</u>W)	How Can I Be Most Useful (in this conversation)? Step #4	Prompt Coachee to Find Solutions Step #5
4. Janos is overloaded with customer work.	Improve work-life balance through better time-management. Why is this important? Missed deadlines; dissatisfied customers; potential burnout.	**Thinking outside the box** is challenging. Feeling of "I don't know how" to change my situation.	The idea of rethinking an entirely new way of working is highly appealing and energizing.	Ask challenging questions to start thinking outside the box *right now*.	**"What advice would you give someone else on this question?"** **"Where could you procure new ideas to dramatically change the way you work?"**
5. Lena Paolo feels stuck and unsatisfied in role.	Exercise more creativity at work. Why is this important? To stay engaged and productive.	**Engage team members to collaborate differently and creatively.**	Expand capacity to influence and build relationship with peers.	Engage with the principles of creative thinking right now by not shooting down any idea, and being expansive.	**"How might you start to influence the team on this topic?"** **"What creative ideas can you think of right now to set different expectations with your peers?"**

The concept of active listening was originally used in the context of therapy, developed by Carl R. Rogers in the late 1960s. It was then integrated as an important communication principle in different "helping professions" (care giving, consulting, coaching) and later to people managers to improve human relationships. Research has confirmed many benefits of active listening, including stress relief, improved empathetic understanding, and unconditional positive regard.[3]

The benefits of active listening with coachees are immediate: A coachee will talk and explore a topic only in relation to the coach's capacity to listen. This is, perhaps, obvious but not to be taken for granted. Workplaces are full of distractions, urgencies, texts, and deadlines. Uninterrupted listening seems a great luxury. Coachees rarely struggle to interrogate their own assumptions unless they feel they've been heard and understood in their current thinking.[4]

A coach uses active listening to help others feel heard and understood, enlarge and enrich the conversation by shedding light on blind spots, and note discrepancies where facts or ideas don't connect:[5]

- Interesting. Does that meet your goal of …?
- I'm curious how that can help you learn?
- I see. Would you enjoy the challenge of that?
- You seem to be most excited about your first idea.

The creative thinking comes from the client's brain, supported by the coach's questions and encouragement.

> It's important to ask thought-provoking questions. Be careful not to offer solutions. When you attempt to solve the coachee's problem, you may actually be delaying their development. Coaching is about supporting your client to find their own solution.
>
> **– Bill Palmer**
> *Certified Facilitator of Manager-as-Coach I*

What if the Coach Is Working Harder than the Client?

After the transition question, the discussion evolves, with the coach using her own curiosity to learn more about the coachee's assumptions with the goal of generating *a set of new options*. This is a time to relax and be expansive. In order to generate a number of ideas, the coach may need to

DIVERGING AND CONVERGING WHILE COACHING

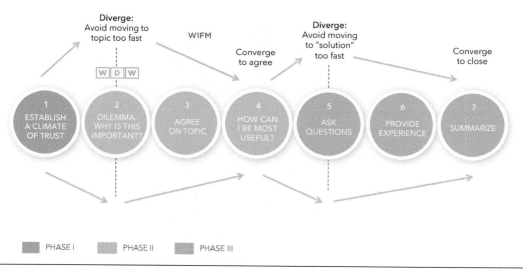

Figure 5.1 The nature of the coach's questions changes based on intent of each step. In Steps #2 and 5, questions tend to be most expansive. In Steps #3, 4, and 7, questions are meant to focus the conversation and test outcomes.

say something like, "That's one interesting idea. What's another way you might approach this?" When a number of ideas have emerged, the coach will ask the client to select one or more ideas with which to experiment. This process of diverging and exploration, followed by coming to a conclusion (converging) during Steps #5 and 6 is much like what happens in Steps #2 and 3. See Figure 5.1.

It's very common that coaches speak entirely too much in Step #5. When the client is searching or even struggling, be patient. The client should be working harder than the coach, signaling the responsibility is on his shoulders. A coach helps by giving time and space for the client to reflect. If nothing emerges, the coach can try a different transition question or two, until one evokes an idea. It's also perfectly OK to have the client reflect and come back with ideas later.

By this point in the model, the client hopefully senses that he's in charge of his own development. He's had the experience in Phase II of deciding what he wants for himself, why he's motivated to do so, and what role he wants the coach to play. If there's any lingering doubt about who will lead the idea-generation required in Step #5, it's up to the coach to now make it very clear. The coach must resolutely avoid giving advice or answers. Even strong requests must be gently refused.

Figure 5.2   Who has the monkey, the coach or client?

"Who has the monkey?" we ask new coaches observing a coaching role-play, meaning "Who is holding the responsibility?"[6] The "monkey" is the metaphor because those arms, legs, and tail can wrap around the coach and stay there (especially in coach-led coaching, or when the coach has been very active in the contracting phrase). The coach can be sure she has the monkey when she's doing the talking and giving advice or ideas. While not always obvious to coaches themselves, outside observers easily detect body language, energy, and words that make it plain when the coach is more invested in the development than the client. In these cases, the monkey has not been transferred (Figure 5.2).

Coaches who keep the monkey, offering "help," do the thinking in lieu of the coachee. This puts the coach in the center when clients should feel highly motivated with their own ideas. Unwittingly, coaches who do the thinking take away the opportunity for clients to feel smart, confident, and capable, which ultimately disempowers the client. They also reduce the likelihood of success – the coach's ideas will be better suited for herself (learning style, skillset, etc.) because what works for the coach won't fully correspond to the coachee. Refuse to be seduced into thinking you know what's best for the client. Instead, toss the responsibility back to the client to think it through himself. Coaches, meanwhile, listen, ask questions, and encourage the client to be expansive in their thinking.

What if the Coach Becomes Confused or Lost?

If the coach becomes confused at any point during the exploration, consider that the coachee is likely to be confused, too. Avoid thinking that you need to figure everything out. Remember, the client should be working harder than you. Consider asking the coachee to sort it out:

a. "Your goal, Julian, is to find ways to become more curious. Are ideas emerging?" (Then, wait for a recalibration on the coachee's part.)
b. "Is this conversation helping you get clear on what you want to experiment with?"
c. "I'm unsure where we are in the conversation, can you summarize where you think we are?"

This is part of the magic of authenticity in coaching – you can be transparent, not have to know it all, and build trust all at the same time.

What if the Client Backs Away or Resists Looking for Solutions?

If the client is hesitant or demonstrates resistance to moving forward, the coach will need to go back to prior step(s) which were not established adequately. She checks again for Trust, Agreement on the Topic, and an attractive WIFM. Examples of going back to a prior step of the model:

a. It sounds like you're not sure that improving your peer relationships is the root cause of your dilemma. Is that right? (testing again for Agreement on the Topic)
b. My goal is not to push you to do something that's not in your interest. My goal is to help you feel more successful and satisfied at work. Is what we're discussing right now important in relation to your other priorities? (testing for WIFM)
c. I'm sensing that you are uneasy or unsure about something and I'm curious about it. Would you share what's on your mind? (testing for Trust)

Challenges of Step #5

- *The coach wants to control the outcome.* Prescribing approaches and solutions defeats the purpose of coaching and constitutes micro-management. When tempted to overrule the client's idea, refrain. Ask about implications, opportunities, and risks. Promoting empowerment, innovation, and creativity means that the coach at times will need to be partially uncomfortable with the ideas presented.
- *The client has no (or few) ideas.* It's not uncommon for clients to say they don't have any ideas in response to the transition question. Sometimes, the client will say, "I'll have to think about that," or "I don't know." In these cases, coaches can either *push* or *pause.*

  Push. "Let's take 5 minutes right now to develop very preliminary thoughts and ideas." This is useful when the client doesn't realize that coaching means taking the time to think about a topic aloud, right now, or when you believe the client might be experiencing mild resistance to moving forward.

  Push. "What would you say if you *did* know?" This was the best retort I ever heard (which was said to me by a coach) to my "I don't know." Sure enough, I found some ideas to start the ball rolling.

  Pause. In some cases, coachees may ask to go away to reflect on the question. Whether it's a lack of time or a learning style preference, there's no rule that the thinking must be done in the presence of the coach. Follow up to hear conclusions and engage again.

  Pause. Sometimes, the ideas generated are too few, too narrow, uninformed, or shortsighted. The coach may want to suggest the coachee gather ideas from others, and come back for a follow-up. The quality of thinking will likely have improved significantly.
- *The client is highly frustrated about his Dilemma.* When the client is motivated to solve the dilemma but is highly frustrated about it (perhaps he feels he's tried everything), try switching Step #6 and Step #5. Moving to Step #6 first is the chance for the coach to jump-start the thinking by sharing a personal story about a similar challenge, provide an analogy, or make a suggestion. The goal, in these cases, is to keep the client engaged because, in that moment, they need support more than challenge. When the client gets curious and the frustration recedes, hand them the monkey again: "What ideas have come to mind for you," or "How could this – or something similar to this – apply in your situation?"

Step #6: Provide Your Experience to Help Guide

A number of years ago, I heard an innovation speaker address a group of engineers on the topic of promoting creative thinking.[7] His main message was more like a tip, but what a tip it was. If you want people to come up with more creative ideas, he said, respond to every new idea with: "What I like about that idea is …" This simple communication technique can be adopted immediately, and is also profound when you consider that great leaders help us feel empowered, intelligent, and creative. Conversely, when managers act as arbiters, permission-givers, and answer-givers, employees learn to be passive. The phrase also captures the essence of what's needed in Step #6 – a response *that builds directly on what the coachee just said in Step #5.*

Step #6 is often delivered with a light touch, so as not to draw too much attention to the coach or introduce the coach's ideas. Instead, the goal is to build directly on what the coachee said in Step #5. Coaches may simply provide support and encouragement, or probe for more ideas or deeper thinking. The manager-coach can also express their concern if they perceive the risk of the idea is too great or is inappropriate in any way. See Table 5.2 for examples.

Challenges of Step #6

- *Responding to ideas from Step #5 with advice.* By expressing advice or a direction, the coach takes the monkey back from the coachee and reinforces the message of doing things "right" instead of prioritizing the learning. Even articulating a preference (such as "I like your second idea" from the table) can indicate subtle permissioning is at play, which works *against* the greater goals of coaching. Whenever possible, *experiment with making fewer evaluative comments.*
- *Storytelling.* Some managers easily fall into telling stories about the past, where they worked, what they achieved, and what they learned. Manager-coaches should consider who is being served in that moment – the client or themselves. Only use (abbreviated) stories if they directly relate to the issue being discussed and can be used to deepen understanding or expand the idea for the coachee (rather than simply agreeing, which can reinforce that the coachee needs to be fully aligned or will not be fully trusted to make his own choices). Have the discipline to share only sparingly, keeping the focus on the client.

Table 5.2   Sample Coach Responses in Step #6

As a conclusion to Step #5, if the client says…	The Coach might say … (Step #6)
"In sum, I think I need to get more information from the factory."	"What I like about that idea is that you're going straight to the source for your information, while at the same time opening the possibility of a better relationship with the operations manager."
"…So those are three ideas I have to manage my time better."	"I especially like your second idea: reducing the number of decisions made each day helps to manage time. Continually asking yourself questions takes a lot of energy."
"I'm fairly convinced I need to call the customer to discuss this."	"I like the fact that your instinct is to communicate with the customer. Tell me about your lingering doubts."
"I have four ideas to try out now."	"Experimenting and failing-fast are ways to stay nimble. Which one will you try first?"
"I have strong feelings about doing it this way…"	"I understand why you might feel that way. And while I have a few concerns, I want you to try out your idea. Will you check back with me in a few days to let me know how it's going?"
"I've decided to send out a memo to the organization about this issue."	"That's one approach that *could* work, but the extended team will have some ideas on this, too. Before doing so, I'd like to request you expand your set of ideas by talking to your peers before you decide. Would you be OK with that?"
"I've tried everything, and I am utterly fed up trying!" (a case where you consider swapping Steps #5 and #6, as mentioned in the last section)	"I can see you've already spent a lot of energy trying to resolve this, which to me means you care about making this work. Thank you for working hard; I'm sorry this has been difficult and frustrating for you." (*Pause to allow for comment from client*) "Would it be helpful if I suggested one or two strategies to stimulate your thinking?"

■ *The coach disagrees with the coachee's conclusions.* An expected concern for coaches in putting the client in the center of his own learning process is that the coach may disagree with the experiments or actions. When the impact of any false step is manageable, probe about downstream effects, but invite the coachee to go forward with their idea. Making mistakes and experiencing failure is an important part of learning. Meanwhile, the coach stays close to the situation and increases coaching time on the topic. When the impact of the idea has serious negative implications in your mind, tell the client you are uncomfortable with the idea and ask the coachee to gather more information or input. Coaches who take the time to explain their concerns transparently take responsibility for their own fears.

Step #7: Summarize. How Do You Feel? Was This Useful?

Beginnings get a lot of our attention: ribbon-cutting ceremonies, kick-offs, welcoming rituals, house-warming parties, grand openings, and so on. But have you ever considered the value or importance of endings? By "endings," I mean how events and conversations end or close. Too often the emphasis on endings is muted, relative to beginnings. And yet, there is much to be reflected upon and learned. One exception is the practice of summarizing. The focus of summarizing tends to be the recitation of action items, which is useful but doesn't replace other important aspects that would be useful to call out. Consider family holidays and what gets said as you stand at the door or walk guests out to their cars saying things *that may never have been uttered* had there not been an ending. Consider an experience leaving a job or company, and the feelings which are exchanged in the last days. What transpires in those ending moments are expressions of appreciation, emotion, final thoughts, summations of the experience and other important messages.

While these examples are perhaps more momentous than the ending of a single coaching conversation, the same principles apply. *The goal of Step #7 is for coachee and coach to learn.* By ending too quickly, the coach over-looks the opportunity to gather valuable information, which includes getting feedback, offers of support, testing of outcomes, and expressions of feelings. Using the analogy of inviting someone to lunch, find out how the meal tasted! Did your guest enjoy himself? Will he come back again?

The Coach Gets Feedback

In our workshops, we have the opportunity after a role-play to ask coach and client how they felt. For one person to feel satisfied and the other to feel entirely the opposite is not uncommon. In real life, incorporating Step #7 is meant to share conclusions and realign as necessary. Taking the extra few minutes tends to benefit the coach as much as, or more than, the coachee. We recommend coaches ask at least two different kinds of questions, so the coach can apply the learnings next time.

In the course of "closing," other needs and topics may emerge. These topics should be named, agreed upon in terms of importance or priority (and why), and scheduled for follow-up.

Sample Closing Questions

What specifically a coach says to close the conversation depends on what has transpired. The coach asks herself what she really wants to know in that moment. Oftentimes, the question comes from a feeling or concern. Always ask *at least* two questions when closing (See Table 5.3).

Challenges of Step #7

- *Managers who only ask for a standard recap might be missing more holistic feedback.* Summarizing is an excellent idea, but experiment with adding one or two other closing questions focused on the person. For example, ask how the coachee feels, in what way the conversation was helpful, or about the coachee's experience being coached. When coaches ask about feelings, responses generally reflect the coachee's entire experience.
- *Skipping the step entirely.* New coaches often seem uncomfortable and tend to close with a quick "thanks." Instead, coaches can invite the client to step outside of the subject matter of Steps #5 and 6 to provide an opening for the coachee to say something he didn't say, which is quite often among the most authentic, valuable comments of the entire conversation.

Bringing It All Together: A Coaching Conversation Steps #1-7

Let's return to our coaching examples – using only key elements – from start to finish, beginning with our strategic account manager, Julian. Again, there are no "correct dialogues"; these are samples of how one scenario might play out through to the end. As before, due to considerations of length and

Table 5.3 Sample Closing Questions for Step #7

Closing Questions	*When to Use*
"Can you summarize what we decided?"	Useful anytime unless the conversation was already straightforward (in which case it may sound pedantic or formulaic)
How do you feel about this conversation?	Useful anytime
What do you see as the first steps?	When there have been a number of actions discussed and you want to ensure the client is clear where to start
Was this helpful?	Useful anytime
Is there anything else you wanted to talk about?	Useful anytime. You sense there may be something else on the coachee's mind and/or have a few extra minutes
Thank you so much for collaborating with me on this. I look forward to seeing how your idea works.	Useful anytime, as long as it's a genuine feeling
What I liked about this conversation is …	Useful anytime
I'm curious what you're more aware of now (that you weren't before we began this discussion)?	Useful anytime
Thanks for sharing with me. Can you give some feedback about one thing you appreciated about this discussion and one thing you wished had been different?	Useful when you want feedback on the coaching process or content
I have a sense that you didn't get what you needed from this conversation.	You feel uneasy about the conversation or how it ended.
(Anything else you're wondering about!)	Be mindful to keep the focus on the client.

complexity, we presuppose that the client *agrees* with the Dilemma, hence there is no separate column for Step #3. The sentence in **bold** is what has been agreed upon (Table 5.4).

By studying the table you can begin to see the *gestalt* of a coaching conversation. While there is also much left out that might transpire "live," these sketches hopefully allow you to detect the model's logic. What's missing, of course, is your own voice and style, which will develop over time with practice.

Table 5.4 Step #1–#7

Presenting Topic	Want (and Why) Step #1 (WDW)	Developmental Dilemma (Step #3 Agreement Is in Bold Step #2 (WDW)	WIFM Step #3 (WDW)	How Can I be Most Useful? Step #4	Prompt Coachee to Find Solutions Step #5	Provide Experience to Help Guide Step #6	Summarize, Was This Useful? How Do You Feel? Step #7
1. Julian is unable to appease Customer Jane.	Manager wants Julian to provide a consistent experience to customers. Why is this important? (1) Happy customers will forgive occasional mistakes and (2) will be more loyal to the brand; (3) Julian becomes a multifaceted resource to the customer.	Julian struggles with how to create an experience, in part because he has trouble thinking of things to talk to them about. **He wants to become more curious.** He has a bias for working with his internal customers who have come to know and respect him over time.	By engaging more with the external customer, Julian gains insights to pass on to his internal customers.	Listen and provide a reaction; role model what curiosity looks like within this conversation.	"What could you do to increase your level of curiosity about Customer Jane?" or … "What do you think your internal customers would like to know about Customer Jane?"	Manager shares his observations about when he sees Julian's curiosity *rise* (to draw more self-awareness; to remind Julian of his current capacity to be curious). or… "Makes sense. And do you think there's anything Customer Jane might like us to know about her?" (expand the client's thinking).	(Use at least 2 "closers" each time) **"Was this conversation useful to you?" "Is there anything you are curious about that you'd like to mention before we close?" "How do you feel after this conversation?" "Thank you for sharing your ideas. What are the next steps?"**

(Continued)

Table 5.4 (Continued) Step #1–#7

Presenting Topic	Want (and Why) Step #1 (WDW)	Developmental Dilemma (Step #3 Agreement Is in Bold) Step #2 (WDW)	WIFM Step #3 (WDW)	How Can I be Most Useful? Step #4	Prompt Coachee to Find Solutions Step #5	Provide Experience to Help Guide Step #6	Summarize, Was This Useful? How Do You Feel? Step #7
2. Diana spends a lot of time on emails and meetings.	Be more strategic; Spend time to reflect and act on issues critical to the business long term. Why is this important? Fire-fighting does not replace long-term solutions.	**Manage expectations of the internal stakeholders** who send many requests for information.	Be seen as an enterprise-wide thinker; become a more visionary leader.	Play devil's advocate to ensure the ideas correspond to the organizational realities.	Have you successfully been able to reshape someone's expectations of you in the past? What did you learn? How can you reshape others' expectations of you to allow time for more strategic initiatives?	"What I like about what you said is that these are big ideas that are strategic, which corresponds to your goal."	**"Was this helpful?"** **"Do you feel these ideas will help you learn more about becoming an enterprise-wide thinker?"**
3. Marcos feels resentful and angry at the R&D director for being so difficult to work with.	Improve relationship with R&D director. Why is this important? Collaboration is not optional; Business results are required.	**Say "no" to those who push too hard or are inflexible.**	Respecting own needs (establishing boundaries) will recalibrate the relationship. Ability to manage conflict will help in all aspects of client's life.	Role-play the conversation, with coach playing R&D director. Client gives feedback about the impact of the behavior.	What did you become aware of as we role-played that conversation? How are you thinking about this now?	"I had a similar reaction when preparing for a difficult conversation. Your clarity while you spoke during the role-play had the impact of wanting to be supportive of you."	**"What are you aware of now that we've discussed this case and practiced a different approach?"**

(Continued)

Table 5.4 (Continued)   Step #1–#7

Presenting Topic	Want (and Why) Step #1 (WDW)	Developmental Dilemma (Step #3 Agreement Is in Bold) Step #2 (WDW)	WIFM Step #3 (WDW)	How Can I be Most Useful? Step #4	Prompt Coachee to Find Solutions Step #5	Provide Experience to Help Guide Step #6	Summarize, Was This Useful? How Do You Feel? Step #7
4. Janos is overloaded with customer work.	Improve work-life balance through a different orientation to time-management. Why is this important? Potential burnout.	**Thinking outside the box is challenging.** A feeling of "I don't know how" to change my situation.	The idea of rethinking an entirely new way of working is highly appealing and energizing.	Ask challenging questions to start thinking outside the box *right now.*	What advice would you give someone else on this question? Where could you procure new ideas to dramatically change the way you work?	"I like that advice. Given how overloaded you are, I wonder how you can take your own advice so that it's both effective *and simple.*"	**"How do you feel as we close?"** **"Can you summarize what you've decided?"** **"What is the first thing you will do to move toward your goal?"**
5. Lena feels stuck and unsatisfied in role.	Exercise more creativity at work. Why is this important? To stay engaged and productive.	**Engage team members to collaborate differently and creatively.**	Expand capacity to influence and build relationship with peers.	Engage with the principles of creative thinking right now by not shooting down any idea, and being expansive.	How might you start to influence the team on this topic? What creative ideas can you think of right now to set different expectations with your peers?	"I like your first idea and think it could be very effective. How could you make that idea even bigger?"	**"What do you see your next steps to be?"** **"What did you like most about the dialogue we've just had?"** **"What should we avoid doing differently next time?"**

Notes

1 Kubota, S., Mishima, N., & Nagata, S. (2004). A study of the effects of active listening on listening attitudes of middle managers. *Journal of Occupational Health, 46* (1), 62.
2 Moen, F., & Kvalsund, R. (2008). What communications or relational factors characterize the method, skills and techniques of executive coaching. *Journal of Coaching in Organizations, 6* (2), 18.
3 Kubota, S., Mishima, N., & Nagata, S. (2004). A study of the effects of active listening on listening attitudes of middle managers. *Journal of Occupational Health, 46* (1), 60–61.
4 Ivey, A. E., & Ivey, M. B. (2006). *Intentional Interviewing and Counseling: Facilitating Client Development in a Multicultural Society* (6th Ed). Emeryville, CA: Wadsworth.
5 Ibid.
6 The metaphor of the monkey comes from a *Harvard Business Review* classic: Oncken, W., & Wass, D. L. (1974). Management time: Who's got the monkey? *Harvard Business Review.*
7 I'm sorry to say I could not locate the name of the speaker.

Chapter 6

Becoming a Manager-Coach

Where attention goes, neural firing flows, and neural connection grows.

— Daniel J. Siegel, MD

Early in my consulting career, I attended a daylong workshop in Phoenix about how to get my workspace organized. The workshop leader, Karen Ussery, left a lasting impression on me. Her main message was that getting organized requires two things: tools and habits. The *tools*, she said, must be both useful and (preferably) enjoyable to look at, touch, and use. The *habits* are behavioral disciplines adhered to over time. The combination makes life easier, calmer, and more productive. "Buy high-quality, beautiful file folders," she said, "and move all papers into them at the end of each day." "Get a labeler, one that has enough features, and use it for anything with hidden contents inside." "For those afraid to delete email, create a folder called 'Probably will never need' for any message you're afraid to delete but doubt you'll ever need again." "Unclutter your top drawer: find your favorite 3 writing instruments and get rid of the rest. Always put those 3 back in the drawer so you know where they are." Karen was a godsend with her model of tools and practices, and helped me look forward to coming into my office.

Tools and Practices

In the case of coaching, you now have a *tool*, the Developmental Coaching Model. What you need now are effective *habits* which support you. What Karen called "habits" are akin to "practices." Practices are the behaviors, habits, and routines that when *sustained* over time, and are *meaningful*, will change your brain (quite literally). Perhaps you've heard that brains are "plastic"? Neuroplasticity, or brain plasticity, refers to the brain's ability to change throughout life. The human brain has the incredible ability to reorganize itself by forming new connections between brain cells when reinforced over time and imprint a new pattern of thinking. This pattern extends to other domains of thinking and acting. The way ecologists, engineers, and attorneys solve non-work-related problems on the weekend is due to the way they've structured their brain as they've studied over time in a particular way. Changing practices – encoding new behaviors, habits, and routines – are key to culture change.[1]

"Meaningful" practices are those which must connect to something deeply valued by the person doing them. These practices might be attributed to an aspect of the person's success. In Karen's case, a professional organizer, cleaning off her desk at the end of the day is more than a good feeling; it's part of her identity. (And this begs the question whether practice makes something meaningful or making something meaningful makes it a practice.)

With this in mind, making any change – in this case, becoming a skilled manager-coach – is connected to what you do every day, and will require integrating new and different practices over time. This last chapter, then, is devoted to practices that can help you make people development part of who you are.

Starting to Coach and Building the Practices

The following ideas are meant to stimulate your own thinking about what you need to jump-start your coaching and to build your skills (and neural connections).

Draft Your Leadership "Bumper Stickers"

A bumper sticker on the back of a vehicle lets others know what the driver feels strongly about. Whether the message concerns politics, families, school, location, or pets, these messages state in very few words what's meaningful to him or her, even if it's the desire to amuse others. In organizations (and life), managers need their own leadership bumper sticker(s) to communicate in simple terms what they're passionate about – a leadership purpose. Doing so provides guidance about expectations and needs, and helps the manager align actions with words. While the thought of bumper stickers may evoke superficiality or frivolity, a manager becoming clear about what she believes is the most powerful action of all as a start to building trust and simplifying decision-making. With your bumper stickers clear in mind, managers can check for the connection to coaching (or learning).

Some already hold their leadership principles closely and can connect them to the themes in this book with little effort, such as:

- Trusting – requires active listening, joining, engaging resistance, having the other's best interest at heart
- Honoring resistance – one's own and others' (it's where change happens)
- Knowing what makes others tick and why (motivation is the engine for change)
- Curiosity leads to learning and growth (psychological flexibility)
- Asking for feedback and finding peer coaches (self-awareness and humility)
- Engaging people in what matters to them (commitment means discretionary effort)

When you find your own words, write them down. Get reactions from those who know you best. Know what you believe in most.

Make No Assumptions; Define Terms

Once you have your bumper stickers, you have an opportunity to engage on the words you've chosen. Especially with diverse teams (different functions, geographies, tenure, life experiences, thought processes), words will evoke different emotions and meanings. "Curiosity" could evoke danger, "coaching" could evoke failure, and "trust" at work could be seen as naive. These discussions are invaluable to help you know others, increase your awareness, and further frame your themes going forward. Subsequently, consider discussions about the current team climate for coaching, in terms of psychological safety, candor, and learning. Seek to develop and maintain learning contracts to make learning an ongoing priority in the team and mutually committing to development in part through coaching.

Walk Yourself through Step #2 of the Model

As you set your intention and goal to become a manager-coach (your want), take time to consider the other two elements in Step #2: your developmental dilemma and WIFM. Quite likely, you have one or more concerns about embracing coaching fully. You may be interested, even intrigued, but perhaps also aware of resistance within you to go full speed ahead. One client, for example, experienced a distaste for generating unnecessary power-distance. By putting himself in the coach role, he felt to be communicating a position of hierarchy or superiority. As we explored, he realized his challenge was leadership courage. Leadership courage, therefore, became a parallel – and complementary – goal to that of becoming a manager-coach.

By using the DCM on yourself (or finding a coach to support), you accelerate your progress and do the same work you'll ask your coachees to do.

Establish the Coaching Expectation of Yourself and Your Direct Reports

Changing course in how you lead or communicate can surprise unsuspecting colleagues, so explicitly describing what you're doing and why can save others time from a lot of wondering. Here's a sample (abbreviated) explanation:

> Team, I'm starting several new practices related to growth and development. You've heard me talk about (innovation/learning/curiosity, etc. – *bumper sticker*), and to that end I will be modifying how I engage with you. You may notice I'll be backing off on giving you advice and, instead, asking more questions. My goal is to become more of a manager-coach. This means me doing things a little differently. To begin, coaching means having conversations to become more aware of how the challenges you face at work connect to your personal and professional development. So for our bi-monthly one-on-one check-in meetings, I'd like to change the structure a bit and make more time to incorporate developmental discussions.

As a practice, you may find taking turns with your direct reports – varying meetings where you bring a topic, then they do, then you do, etc. – works very well to share responsibility for communicating and provides opportunities for each person to set the agenda.

Reframe the Purpose of Coaching When Necessary

In some contexts, the challenge of beginning to coach others is less a matter of interpersonal trust than it is of regional culture. A client near Paris, for example, explained that providing feedback (the theory), and a feature of coach-led coaching, is not at all the norm. Instead, there are clever, but vague, ways to avoid any scent of a deficit such as "Some are much better at that." By introducing a new set of leadership principles, however, the manager-coach was able to bring coaching into his team's practices quite successfully.

In another example, a German client explained that managers should not ask questions of their subordinates that they, themselves, don't know the answer to. The assumption in these cases is that holding a position with a larger scope of responsibility reflects superior thinking and experience, no matter the topic. Managers can lose credibility when they expose a lack of knowing. In these cases, managers find that if they reframe the basic assumptions about coaching and educate others on its purpose and usefulness, it has become acceptable practice. As a strategy to reframe, examine why the exact opposite argument is also true and find examples as analogies.

Establish Metrics

A primary concern for new coaches is dedicating adequate time. A CEO client challenges his people to the "calendar test." Compare what you are doing all day – what's on the calendar – with what has true meaning to you. If developing others is part of your purpose (or you want it to be), there should be proof on the calendar.

To save time in the coaching conversation itself, be ready. Spend time thinking through WDW ahead of time:

a. *Want.* What is the want or need you have and how does that connect to the coachee?
b. *Developmental dilemma.* What different need do you believe may be working at cross-purposes? What's your *theory* about what other want is at play? (If the issue is a symptom, what's the bigger issue that should be addressed?)
c. *WIFM.* What's the benefit for the client to develop? (Ensure this corresponds with what motivates them.) (WIFM)
d. *Trust.* Is trust an issue between you? If so, how will you address this?

Keep the Feedback Loop Going

While completing Step #7 encourages feedback at the end of each conversation, coaching feedback from one's direct reports can also be gathered in a short survey or through one-on-one interviews from time to time.

While surveys collect more candid feedback, one-on-one conversations provide more context and easy follow-up. Sample survey questions below come from Karen Soderberg-Hinchcliffe, Certified Facilitator of workshops Manager-as-Coach I and II:

- Do I have the opportunity to have meaningful conversations and coaching about my work, at work?
- Is the coaching I receive valuable and supportive of my development?
- When I have a conversation – labeled "coaching" or not – is there sufficient structure that the dialogue can be constructive?
- Does my manager reach out and/or make readily available the opportunity to coach or be coached on something important to me and our business?
- Am I well received when I ask for counsel or coaching?
- Do I feel encouraged to coach and be coached?
- Is the climate in my work group and the work environment supportive of the candor required for meaningful conversations?

Other Supportive Practices

There are other major and minor practices to support oneself to develop new coaching skills. Consider these questions:

- Who could you bring along in your coaching journey? Who could become a peer coach? Do you want a professional coach? (There's a wisdom in coaching circles that to *be* an effective coach requires *having* one.)
- Can you post articles on internal and external social media platforms about topics core to your purpose, in relation to coaching?
- Have you posted the DCM in your office or displayed it for easy access?
- Importantly, can you work to embed the DCM into the organization's current processes, making it part of everyone's employee development discussions?

Variations of Coaching

I remember years ago returning from a personal development experience which included work on the topic of being attentive and present to others.

Back at home, I continued the practice everywhere I could … until I realized I was exhausting myself.

My sudden burnout reminded me that I needed to be intentional about who was getting my energy, how long, and when. Similarly, it's very common that those new to coaching will want to apply it in every situation, even when they needn't. Below are two scenarios to consider.

Performance Problems

Among the most common questions is whether to use the DCM when there is a performance problem. The simple answer: Always try to coach, but be clear with the client from the beginning that there *is* a performance issue. Coaches need to remember that they are exercising their hierarchical power when bringing up the word "performance," and it should be used with caution. In English in the United States, simply using the word "performance" can be heard as "this is serious and your job is at risk." So, when coaching someone where there is a serious performance issue, coaches may not have – or need – agreement on the topic, but should try. If manager-coaches can re-engage the coachees through coaching, that is a wonderful outcome and a testament to your coaching.

Problem-Solving With a Coaching Mindset

Sometimes it's impossible to take the time to coach in a given moment. How you respond to a question directed to you can reflect elements of coaching. One option is to use only Steps #2, 4, and 5, which means quickly defining the want, agreeing on the role of the manager-coach, and asking the client how they think best to proceed. It sounds like this:

Coachee: "The approval process is moving too slowly and I don't want to step on any toes by moving forward. That said, I need to send this payment out." (Coachee is indicating he wants a quick answer, reaction, or permission to send out the payment.)

Coach: "I understand. It seems you want to send the payment and you want to respect the approval process. You are managing several things at once." (Coach shapes the issue into a dilemma, and at the same time checking for understanding. He is also surprised to receive this solicitation for approval when the coachee has the authority to decide, and makes a mental note for future coaching.

When the coachee confirms "yes" to his statement, the coach continues.)

Coach: "How can I be useful right now?" (Skipping to Step #4, the coach prompts the client to be clear about what kind of support he really needs.)

Coachee: "Do you think it's fine to go ahead and send payment?" (Coach recognizes he is looking for simple advice, but redirects to Step #5.)

Coach: "You've been thinking about this. What does your experience suggest here?" (Step #5)

Coachee: "I'm fairly certain this scenario calls for me to go ahead and send the payment. I'll talk it through with the finance manager tomorrow."

Coach: "OK. Let me know how it goes." (Coach may have a point of view but sees more can be learned by letting the coachee decide. Coach makes a note if he sees a pattern of the coachee relying on others to make the tough calls.)

The formal and informal practices presented in this chapter help the brain change. Habits and behaviors repeated over time – which are also held as deeply meaningful – create new, neural pathways. When the manager-coach learns to fuse the business needs to people development, she becomes a force multiplier. She serves her coachees above all while also supporting business success and sustainability. For the manager-coach, there is the great satisfaction of inspiring others while bringing more care and humanity to the workplace.

Notes

1 White, D. G. (2017). *Rethinking Culture: Embodied Cognition and the Origin of Culture in Organizations*. New York, NY: Routledge.